The Heaven Question

What People Really Believe About Heaven When No One Is Listening

Shehzad Amlani

ISBN: 9798903840908

Dedication

For my family,

who helped me research and answer the questions I could not answer, who was patient with me when I couldn't give them time because I was writing this book.

Acknowledgment

This book exists because more than two hundred people trusted me with their most private thoughts about death and meaning. Most cannot be named, but each shaped these pages in ways that matter deeply. You know who you are. Thank you for your honesty, your time, and your willingness to say what you actually think instead of what you are supposed to say.

To the Rabbis, Priests, Imams, and Buddhist teachers who gave so generously of their time and insight, thank you for your patience with my questions and with my gaps in understanding.

To the hospice nurses and end-of-life care professionals who welcomed me into sacred spaces and trusted me with their observations, thank you for the work you do and for the wisdom you shared.

To the early readers who sat with messy drafts and told me what was not working, this book is stronger because of your candor.

To my family, who lived with two years thinking out loud about death and somehow remained patient through all of it.

To my children, who asked questions I could not answer and deserved better than easy phrases.

And to Margaret, who began all of this with one question I still cannot fully answer, but now understand differently.

The insights in this book belong to everyone who shared their truth with me.

The gaps and limitations belong entirely to me.

Author's Note

I am not a hospice nurse, theologian, or religious scholar. I am a writer who became fascinated by how ordinary people talk about heaven after the death of a close friend.

This book is based on more than two hundred conversations conducted over two years. I spoke with clergy, hospice staff, dying patients, grieving families, and scholars across multiple traditions. This is not a scientific study or a representative survey. I did not randomly sample Americans. I spoke with people I could reach, primarily in the Chicago area and almost entirely in English, through personal networks and religious communities willing to participate.

Who are missing from these pages matters. You will find limited representation of Black Protestant traditions, Pentecostal Christianity, rural perspectives, working-class voices, and Global South expressions of faith. You will find almost nothing about Indigenous cosmologies, and only brief encounters with non-Abrahamic traditions such as Hinduism and Buddhism. My access was shaped by my networks, my geography, and my language.

A note on composites. Many individuals described in this book are composite characters who represent patterns that appeared across multiple conversations. When you encounter a named character, assume they are composite unless I state otherwise. For example, Linda in Chapter 4 represents a pattern I observed among several women who expressed certainty in church while privately doubting. Her words are reconstructed from notes, but her belief and situation are real. In contrast, Margaret in Chapter 1 is one actual person, with identifying details changed.

These composites protect privacy and help maintain narrative clarity. When an anecdote feels unusually complete, it often reflects similar moments shared by more than one person.

Some dialogue has been condensed or reconstructed from notes taken at the time. All names and identifying details have been changed throughout.

You can trust that every belief described is real, every pattern emerged from actual conversations, and every synthesis reflects what I genuinely heard.

This book represents one writer's attempt to understand, not to persuade. It is not intended as religious, medical, legal, or therapeutic advice.

I cannot tell you what happens after death. No one can.

What I can share is what people told me when I asked them to speak honestly, rather than repeating the language we all learn to use.

A Note On Methods And Limitations

Over two and a half years, I conducted 213 conversations about heaven and death. This section explains how I found participants who are missing, and what those absences mean for the patterns described here.

How I Found People

I began with personal networks. Friends introduced me to family members who were willing to talk. Colleagues connected me with people they thought might have meaningful perspectives. I reached out to religious leaders and asked whether anyone in their communities wanted to participate. Several hospice organizations agreed to ask patients if they were open to speaking with me. I also posted requests in online forums. At times, I simply sat in coffee shops and started conversations.

This was not random sampling.

It was snowball sampling. Each conversation often led to others who shared similar backgrounds, beliefs, or social circles. My network shaped who I was able to reach.

Who Are Missing

This matters because the sample has clear limitations.

Within these pages, you will find:

Limited representation of Black Protestant traditions and Black church life.

Few Pentecostal or charismatic Christian voices.

Almost no rural or working-class perspectives.

Light coverage of Global South Christianity and Islam.

Minimal engagement with Indigenous cosmologies.

No traditions that would have required languages I do not speak.

Most interviewees were urban or suburban, primarily educated, and largely middle-class or above. All conversations were conducted in English. Most took place in the Chicago metropolitan area.

What This Means

The patterns described in this book are real, but they reflect a specific slice of American religious life in the early 2020s.

A different writer, working in a different place and with different access, would almost certainly encounter different beliefs and different themes.

I am not claiming to describe what all Americans believe about heaven.

I am describing what I found when I asked the people, I could reach to tell me the truth.

The beliefs are theirs.

The synthesis is mine.

The limitations are real.

Contents

PART I:
THE SILENCE AND THE SCRIPT

Chapter 1
The Silence After Margaret

Margaret died on a Tuesday.

Not dramatically, not in a way that made the universe pause or the cosmos take notice that someone important had just left. She died in a hospice bed in Evanston, morphine managing the pain while cancer finished what it had started six months earlier.

She was seventy-three. We had known each other for fifteen years, the kind of friendship that forms in adulthood, when you meet someone who thinks the way you think, understands your references, and can finish your arguments better than you can.

Margaret was sharp. She could diagnose organizational dysfunction in three questions, dismantle a bad business plan in two minutes, and explain exactly where your logic failed without making you feel stupid for missing it.

She had been a consultant. Systems thinking. Process improvement. Work that sounds dry until you watch someone like Margaret do it and rcalize she was really teaching people how to see clearly.

When she got sick, she approached it the same way she

approached everything else, with precision, research, and an unflinching assessment of probabilities. She had stage IV pancreatic cancer. The statistics were not ambiguous. Six months, maybe nine if chemotherapy worked better than expected.

It worked about as well as expected.

By month five, she was in hospice. By month six, she was barely conscious most days.

I visited on a Thursday afternoon in October. She was awake, which had become rare. The morphine kept her comfortable but distant, as if she were watching the world through fog.

We talked about small things. The weather. Her grandchildren. A book she had been reading before she became too tired to focus.

Then she asked a question I was not ready for.

"Do you actually believe that?"

"Believe what?"

"Heaven. Do you actually believe I'm going to heaven?"

For weeks I had been saying comforting things. The standard script. You'll be at peace. You'll see your husband again. You'll be in a better place. I thought I was helping.

But now she was asking me directly whether I believed what

I had been saying, and I realized that I did not.

I had been performing comfort, repeating phrases I assumed she needed to hear. But I did not believe them. Not really.

I believed she was dying. I believed that in six weeks, or six days, she would be gone. I believed her body would stop functioning, her consciousness would end, and she would cease to exist in any form I could recognize.

But I could not say that to her.

So I lied.

"Yes. I believe you're going to heaven."

She looked at me for a long moment, then closed her eyes.

"You're a terrible liar," she said.

We sat in silence after that.

She died nine days later.

I could not stop thinking about that moment. About how I had failed her by not being honest. About how the script had gotten in the way of a real connection. About how I did not actually know what I believed about heaven, because I had never forced myself to examine it.

I had absorbed the language everyone uses. The phrases spoken at funerals. The things said to people who are dying. The comforting ideas about the afterlife that soften the terror of death.

But Margaret had asked me to be honest, and I had given her the script instead.

A month after the funeral, I began asking other people what they believed. Not what they were supposed to believe according to religion, upbringing, or philosophy, but what they actually believed when they thought about death.

I started with a priest. I assumed he would be certain. That was his job, after all, to know these things and to provide answers.

We met in his office at a Catholic church in Oak Park. He was fifty-eight and had been a priest for thirty-two years. I asked him what he believed happened after death.

He leaned back in his chair and was quiet for a moment.

"Honestly?" he said.

"Yes."

"I don't know."

"You don't know?"

"I have faith. I believe in the resurrection. I believe in eternal life. But do I know what that actually means? Do I know what heaven is, or what it feels like, or whether I will recognize myself there? No. I don't know any of that."

"But you tell people you know."

"I tell people what the Church teaches. I give them the tradition. The language. The hope. Whether I know it is literally true is a different question."

"Does that feel dishonest?"

He thought for a moment.

"Sometimes. But certainty is not the same thing as faith. Faith is believing without knowing. If I knew for certain, it would not be faith anymore. It would just be knowledge."

If anyone was going to be certain that heaven did not exist, I assumed it would be a neuroscientist.

I found one. Dr. Sarah was forty-three and had spent fifteen years studying consciousness, brain death, and the neural correlates of awareness. We met in her lab, MRI scans glowing on the screens behind her.

I asked, "So when we die, that's it. Lights out. Nothing."

She leaned back and considered the question.

"Probably."

"Probably?"

"Everything we know suggests consciousness is generated by the brain. When brain activity stops, consciousness appears to stop as well. That's what the data shows. So yes, you are probably done."

"But you said probably."

"We don't actually understand consciousness. We can observe brain activity. We can identify patterns. But we don't know why any of it produces subjective experience. We don't know why there is an 'I' in here, looking out. And if we don't understand consciousness itself, we cannot say with certainty what happens to it when the brain stops."

"So there might be something after death?"

"I'm saying I don't know. And anyone who claims certainty either way is overstating their case."

After those first two conversations, I began to notice a pattern.

Nearly everyone fell into one of two groups. People who claimed certainty but could not explain it, and people who admitted uncertainty but felt guilty about it.

Religious participants would say, "Of course I believe in heaven," and then immediately qualify it. "I don't know what it looks like." "The Bible says this, but I've always wondered." "My church teaches that, but honestly…"

Nonreligious participants would say, "There's obviously

nothing after death," and then pause. "Although sometimes I wonder." "The evidence suggests no, but…" "Rationally I know it isn't real, but when my mother died…"

Nobody was actually certain.

They simply performed certainty because that was what their role required.

Over the next two years, I conducted two hundred and thirteen conversations about heaven and death. What I was documenting, I eventually realized, was not a map of heaven.

It was a map of what people needed heaven to be.

And those turned out to be very different things.

Chapter 2
What I Thought I'd Find

I thought I would find a clean divide.

Believers on one side. Atheists on the other. A clear line separating people of faith from people who relied on reason.

I expected believers to offer theological explanations grounded in scripture and tradition. I expected atheists to cite neuroscience and the absence of evidence.

I assumed I could map it all out. Document the positions. Understand the landscape.

I was wrong about almost everything.

The first month of interviews taught me that stated beliefs and actual beliefs are often very different things.

People's real beliefs were fluid, contradictory, and deeply personal. They changed with age. They shifted with grief. They evolved with experience.

The religious often met communal expectations.

The atheists often met intellectual ones.

Everyone else improvised.

What surprised me most was not the uncertainty itself. It was how rarely it seemed to trouble anyone.

As long as the question remained abstract, people lived comfortably with not knowing. They held contradictions without strain. They could believe in heaven on Sunday and avoid thinking about it for the rest of the week.

But the moment I asked them to explain what they believed and why, discomfort surfaced immediately.

Because saying “I don’t know” out loud feels like failure.

Like you should have figured this out by now.

Like everyone else already has the answer.

Like you are the only one still searching.

But that was the illusion.

Everyone was searching. They had simply learned not to admit it.

I interviewed a hospice chaplain named David who had sat with dying patients for eighteen years. He had prayed with hundreds of people in their final hours and offered comfort about heaven to countless families.

I asked him what he actually believed.

“I believe heaven exists. I have to believe that. Otherwise, this work would destroy me."

"But do you know it exists?"

He looked out the window.

"No. I don't know. I've seen things I can't explain. Moments of peace that seem to come from somewhere beyond the room. Patients who describe seeing deceased loved ones just before they die. But I don't know whether those experiences point to heaven or simply show how the brain behaves as it shuts down."

"So you believe because you need to?"

"I believe because belief makes me more effective at what I do. Whether it is objectively true or not, it functions as truth in my work. It helps people die with less fear. That matters more to me than whether I can defend it philosophically."

I met an oncologist named Dr. Rebecca who treated terminal cancer patients. She was not religious and described herself as agnostic, leaning atheist.

When patients asked her what she thought happened after death, she did not tell them there was nothing.

"I tell them I don't know. And I tell them that uncertainty is acceptable. Not knowing does not mean there is nothing. It only means we cannot know from this side."

"Do you think there might actually be something?"

"Honestly? Probably not. My training tells me consciousness is brain activity, and when the brain stops, consciousness stops. But I have also watched people die peacefully after someone told them it was okay to let go, that their deceased spouse was waiting. And I cannot bring myself to take that from them just to preserve my intellectual honesty."

"Does that feel dishonest?"

"It feels like mercy."

I interviewed a philosophy professor named Dr. James who taught courses on death and dying. He had read every major work on the subject. Epicurus. Heidegger. Nagel. Parfit.

He told me he had concluded that death was simply the end.

"There is no evidence for consciousness continuing. No mechanism by which it could continue. The simplest explanation is that when the brain stops, you stop. Everything else is wishful thinking."

"Are you certain?"

"As certain as I can be about anything I cannot directly observe. Which means I could be wrong. But I am not hedging. I genuinely believe death is the end."

"Does that frighten you?"

"It used to. When I was younger, the idea of nonexistence

terrified me. But the more I thought about it, the more I realized I would not be there to experience it. There is no self left to suffer the absence. So what is there to fear?"

"What about meaning? If everything ends, does anything matter?"

"That question assumes meaning must be permanent to count. But a sunset matters even though it fades. A conversation matters even though it ends. Love matters even though people die. Impermanence does not erase meaning. It simply makes meaning temporal instead of eternal."

What I was discovering was that people organized their beliefs about death around what they needed those beliefs to do.

The chaplain needed heaven in order to function in his work.

The oncologist needed uncertainty so she could offer mercy.

The philosopher needed endings to be acceptable because that is what the evidence suggested.

Each had constructed a framework that allowed them to live with death, their own and others', without collapsing under its weight.

And each believed they were being honest, even when their certainty looked nothing like anyone else's.

I met a woman named Teresa at a grief support group in

Naperville. Her husband had died two years earlier from a heart attack. He was fifty-six.

She told me she believed he was in heaven.

"How do you know?"

"I feel him sometimes. Small things. A song on the radio. A smell that reminds me of him. Moments when I know he is there."

"Do you think that is actually him, or your brain creating comforting associations?"

She looked at me as if the question missed the point.

"It does not matter. If it helps me survive losing him, if it allows me to keep loving him even though he is gone, then it is real enough."

"But you said you believe he is in heaven. Not that it is a useful metaphor. You said you believe it."

"I do believe it. And I also know I believe it because I need to. Both things can be true."

By the end of the first month, my original assumption was gone.

I had thought people's stated beliefs would reflect their actual beliefs.

What I found instead was that most people had constructed

beliefs that served psychological and social purposes first, and pursued truth second.

Or perhaps they had found a way to make truth and function the same thing.

The devout needed certainty to sustain faith.

The skeptics needed uncertainty to preserve intellectual integrity.

The grieving needed continuation in order to survive loss.

And almost no one was willing to admit that their belief might be shaped more by need than by knowing.

What I was documenting was not a map of heaven.

It was a map of how people survive the knowledge of death.

And I was about to discover that children understand this more clearly than anyone.

Chapter 3
What Children See

The first child I interviewed was seven years old.

Her name was Emma. Her grandfather had died three months earlier. Her parents thought it might help her to talk to someone outside the family about what she was feeling and what she believed.

We sat at their kitchen table with crayons and paper. I asked her to draw heaven.

She drew a house with a huge yard. Trees everywhere. A swing set. A dog that looked like a golden retriever.

"Is that your grandpa's house?" I asked.

"No," she said. "It is Max's house."

"Who is Max?"

"My dog. He died last year. He is in heaven now."

"What about your grandpa?"

She thought about that for a moment, then added another house to the drawing. Smaller. Off to the side.

"He is there," she said, pointing. "But mostly he visits Max."

"Why mostly?"

"Because Max missed me a lot when he died. So Grandpa takes care of him until I get there."

I asked if her grandpa and Max were happy in heaven.

"Oh yeah," she said. "Max gets to run and play all day. And nobody yells at him. And there are squirrels."

"Squirrels?"

"Max loved chasing squirrels."

Then she stopped coloring and looked up at me with a question I was not ready for.

"If Max is in heaven, and Max chases squirrels, are there squirrels in heaven for him to chase?"

"I think so," I said.

"But then the squirrels get caught. Do they go to heaven too?"

"Well, yes."

"So do they want to be chased? Or do they get a heaven where they do not get chased?"

I sat there realizing a seven-year-old had just identified the central logical problem with every version of heaven ever imagined.

Whose happiness wins when conflict arises?

Her mother stepped in with something about everyone being happy in their own way, but Emma was not satisfied.

"That does not make sense," she said. "Max cannot be happy without chasing squirrels. Squirrels cannot be happy being chased. Somebody has to be sad. Or Max is not really Max anymore. Or the squirrels are not really squirrels."

She went back to coloring.

Her drawing now had a border of question marks.

Another child, a six-year-old named Ben, told me his dog definitely went to heaven.

"How do you know?" I asked.

"Because that is the rule."

"Who made that rule?"

He looked at me like I was the dumbest adult he had ever met.

"God made it," he said slowly, as if explaining something obvious to someone very slow. "Or maybe the dogs made it. I do not know. But it is definitely a rule because heaven would not be fair without dogs."

I had not planned to interview children.

But after that conversation with Emma, I began asking

parents if their kids would talk to me. Over the next six months, I spoke with forty-three children between the ages of five and twelve.

What I found was this.

Children do not inherit their parents' theology.

They invent their own.

And their inventions reveal things adults spend decades learning to hide.

Most children described heaven as a perfected version of life.

Not a different realm. Not a spiritual dimension. Just this world, but better.

A nine-year-old named Marcus told me heaven was like his house, except bigger. With more rooms. And a pool. And his dad was not tired all the time.

"Does everyone get a house like that?" I asked.

"I think so. Everyone gets what they need."

"What if what you need is different from what someone else needs?"

He paused.

"I guess everyone gets their own heaven," he said. "Like Minecraft. Everyone has their own world."

That metaphor came up again and again.

Heaven as a creative mode. Unlimited resources. No threats. You could build whatever you wanted, and nothing could destroy it.

One girl, age eight, explained it this way.

"In regular life, bad things happen and you cannot stop them. In heaven, you are the admin. You control everything."

"So you are like God in your own heaven?"

"I guess. Or maybe God makes you the admin because you died and that is sad, so he wants you to be happy."

She paused.

"But if everyone is the admin of their own place, then it is not really together, is it? It is just everyone alone in their perfect place."

She looked uneasy.

"Maybe sometimes you can visit," she added. "Like multiplayer."

I asked another child, a seven-year-old named Zara, what happened to people who were mean.

"They have to go to the boring room," she said.

"The boring room?"

"Yeah. Where mean people go. Not forever. Just until they learn."

"What is the boring room like?"

She shrugged. "Boring. Maybe you have to watch educational videos or something."

She said this with the gravity of someone describing the worst possible punishment.

"But not forever," she added. "Just until you get it."

Children who had lost someone recently gave different answers than children who had not.

Children with living grandparents described heaven as something far away. A reward. A place you went after a long life well lived.

Children who had lost parents or siblings described heaven as a repair.

A place where what was taken could be returned.

I met a six-year-old named Lily whose baby brother had died two days after birth. She had never met him, but she drew him constantly. In her pictures, he was always older. Four or five. Running beside her.

"Is that what he looks like in heaven?" I asked.

"Yes," she said. "He gets to grow up there. And when I die, he will be older than me, so he can show me around."

"What will he show you?"

"Where the toys are. Where Mom is. All the good stuff."

She believed her mother was already in heaven, even though her mother was alive and sitting in the next room.

I asked her about that later, carefully.

"Your mom is not in heaven. She is here."

"I know," she said. "But the heavenly part of her is there. Taking care of my brother."

"What is the heaven part?"

"The part that does not have to be sad anymore."

Children also invented solutions to theological problems adults had long abandoned as unsolvable.

A ten-year-old named David told me his grandmother had Alzheimer's before she died. She had not recognized him for the last two years of her life.

"Is she better in heaven?" I asked.

"Yeah. Her brain works again. She remembers everything."

"How do you know?"

"Because heaven fixes things. That is the point."

"What if she liked who she was, even with Alzheimer's?"

He looked at me as if the question made no sense.

"Nobody likes Alzheimer's. It is a bad thing. Heaven takes away bad things."

"What about people who are blind? Do they see in heaven?"

"If they want to."

"What if being blind is part of who they are?"

"Then they can choose. Heaven gives you choices."

This pattern appeared again and again.

Children solved contradictions with flexibility.

Heaven could be anything. God could do anything. The rules bent to make room for every conflict.

Adults, having wrestled with those conflicts for years, knew it was not that simple.

But children had not yet learned to worry about consistency.

The most unsettling conversations were with children who did not believe in heaven but were pretending to for their parents' sake.

I met a twelve-year-old named Sophia whose father had died of cancer eight months earlier. Her mother was devoutly Catholic. They attended Mass every week. They prayed the rosary together.

When I spoke with Sophia alone, she told me the truth.

"I do not think my dad is in heaven."

"Why not?"

"Because it does not make sense. If he is in heaven and he is happy, then he does not miss us. But if he misses us, then he is not happy. So either way, it is not really him anymore."

"Have you told your mom that?"

"No. She needs to believe he is in heaven. It helps her."

"What do you need?"

She thought for a long time.

"I need him to not be dead. But I cannot have that. So I guess I do not need anything."

Twelve years old, and already protecting a parent's grief.

Already learning that sometimes love means hiding what you believe is true.

What children revealed, again and again, was this.

Heaven is not a fixed doctrine passed down intact through

generations.

It is a story we build to solve the problem of loss.

And the story changes depending on what kind of loss we are trying to survive.

Children who lost pets needed heaven to include animals.

Children who lost siblings needed heaven to allow growing up.

Children who lost grandparents needed heaven to make old bodies young again, or at least painless.

Every version of heaven was a response to a specific absence.

Every version was an architecture of longing, built to fill a particular space.

Children, because they had not yet learned to disguise desire as theology, revealed that process clearly.

Adults did the same thing.

We simply used better language.

The last child I interviewed was an eleven-year-old boy named Isaiah.

I asked him what he thought heaven was like.

"I do not know," he said. "But I hope it is whatever my mom needs it to be."

"What does your mom need?"

"She needs my dad to still exist somewhere. So I hope he does."

"Do you think he does?"

He looked out the window for a moment.

"I think he exists in the place where we remember him," he said. "And maybe that is all heaven is. The place in our heads where people do not die all the way."

"That is a very mature way to think about it."

"My therapist helped me with that," he said.

Eleven years old.

In therapy.

Already wrestling with grief. Already learning that belief is as much about the believer as it is about the belief itself.

What children taught me was this.

Adults think we teach children about heaven.

But children show us what heaven is for.

It is a story we tell to make death less terrifying.

A place we imagine so love does not have to end.

Before doctrine, before philosophy, before centuries of debate, children understand something simple.

Heaven is not about truth.

It is about need.

And sometimes the need is so deep that even seven-year-olds will build entire worlds to meet it.

Even worlds bordered by question marks.

Chapter 4

At The Edge

The hospice wing smells like cleaning solution trying to cover something it cannot quite hide. Not death exactly. More like the administrative reality of death. Paperwork, procedures, plastic mattress covers. I had been in hospitals plenty of times, but hospice was different. Regular hospitals pretend you might get better. Hospice has given up pretending.

I was there to meet Sharon, a hospice nurse who had worked in palliative care for seventeen years. A friend from my college days had connected us after I mentioned I was talking with people about heaven.

“You want to know what people really believe?” she had said. “Talk to Sharon. She’s heard every deathbed confession, every last-minute conversion, every final doubt. If anyone knows what people actually think when they’re out of time, it’s her.”

Sharon met me in the break room. She was in her fifties, tired in a way that suggested the fatigue was permanent, and she had the kind of face that made you want to tell her things. We sat with terrible coffee, and I asked what people say about heaven when they are dying.

"Depends on the day," she said. "And who's in the room."

"What do you mean?"

"I mean people die differently depending on their audience. If their pastor is there, they die religious. If their atheist son is there, they die pragmatic. If they're alone, they die honest."

That stopped me.

"So what do they say when they're alone?"

She took a long sip of coffee, as if deciding how much truth I could handle.

"Most of them just say they're tired. Not existentially tired. Physically tired. Ready to stop. Then they ask practical questions. Will it hurt? How long? Can you make sure my daughter doesn't see me like this? The big metaphysical stuff almost never comes up."

"Never?"

"I didn't say never. I said almost never. And when it does come up, it's usually not what you'd expect."

Sharon told me about a man named Robert. Seventy-three. Prostate cancer. Two weeks to live. His family was evangelical, the kind where everyone spoke fluent King James and referred to God's plan with absolute confidence.

They had camped in his room for days, praying, reading

scripture, assuring him that Jesus was waiting, that heaven was prepared, that his mansion was ready.

Robert nodded through all of it. Said amen at the right moments. Held their hands while they prayed.

Then one night, around two in the morning, when everyone had finally gone home to sleep, he pressed the call button.

Sharon went in expecting a pain issue.

Instead, Robert looked at her and said, "I don't know if I believe any of it."

She sat down. "Any of what?"

"Heaven. Jesus. The mansion. Any of it. I've been saying I believe it for fifty years. But I don't know if I actually do. And now I'm about to find out, and I'm terrified that I've been wrong."

Sharon asked whether he wanted to speak with his pastor.

"God, no," he said. "He'd just tell me I'm being tested. That doubt is Satan. That I need to have faith. I don't need faith. I need someone to tell me the truth."

"What truth?"

"Is there anything after this? Or is it just nothing?"

Sharon said she sat there for a long time, trying to figure out what to say to a man with two weeks left who was asking her to solve the fundamental metaphysical question of human existence at two in the morning in a hospice wing in suburban Illinois.

Finally, she said, "I don't know. Nobody knows. But I've been doing this for seventeen years, and I can tell you this. The people who die easiest aren't the ones who are certain. They're the ones who make peace with not knowing."

Robert thought about that.

"How do you make peace with not knowing?"

"You stop waiting for certainty and start deciding what you hope for instead."

He died nine days later. His family was there. The pastor was there. Everyone prayed. Everyone said the right things. According to Sharon, Robert smiled, nodded, and played his part.

But the night before he died, he called her in again.

"I decided."

"Decided what?"

"What I hope for. I hope my wife is okay after I'm gone. I hope my kids remember me as someone who tried. And I hope, if there's anything after this, it's just rest. I'm so tired. I don't need a mansion. I just want to rest."

Sharon said it was the most honest deathbed confession she

had ever heard. No angels. No golden streets. No theological certainty.

Just this: I'm tired, and I hope there's rest.

I asked whether most people died like that, quietly uncertain but trying to hold it together for their families.

"A lot of them do," she said. "But not all. Some people get more certain as they get closer. And that's almost worse."

"Worse how?"

"Because you can't tell if it's a genuine belief or just terror management. Like their brain knows what's coming and cranks up certainty as a survival mechanism."

She told me about a woman named Helen. Sixty-eight. Lung cancer. A lifelong atheist.

Helen had been clear about her beliefs her entire life. No God. No heaven. No afterlife. Death was biological. Consciousness was brain activity. When the brain stopped, you stopped. End of story.

She had explained all of this calmly, the way you might explain how a carburetor works.

Then, three days before she died, something shifted.

Helen began talking about her mother.

"She's here," she said. "In the corner. She's waiting for me."

Sharon assumed it was the morphine. Hallucinations are common at the end. The brain does strange things as it shuts down.

But Helen was insistent.

"I know you think I'm hallucinating. I thought that too at first. But she's really here. And she's telling me it's okay. That there's something after."

Sharon asked whether this changed what she believed.

Helen laughed, which turned into a cough, which took a while to settle.

"I have no idea what I believe anymore. For sixty-eight years I was certain there was nothing. Now I'm seeing my dead mother in the corner of a hospice room, and either I'm hallucinating or I was wrong about everything. Either way, certainty is off the table."

"Does that scare you?"

"Terrifies me," she said. "But also kind of relieving. I spent my whole life thinking I had it figured out. Turns out I didn't. Nobody does. At least now I don't have to pretend."

Helen died two days later. Her daughter was there, holding her hand. According to her daughter, Helen's last words were, "Oh. Well, that's interesting."

Sharon had no idea what she meant.

I spent three months interviewing hospice workers and chaplains. The pattern was clear. People do not die the way they lived. Or rather, they do, but not in the way you would expect.

The religious do not die certain. The atheists do not die doubtful. Everyone, at the end, seems to enter a strange liminal space where the old categories stop working.

A rabbi told me that in thirty years of sitting with dying congregants, almost no one asked about heaven.

"They ask about their families," he said. "Their legacies. Whether they were good enough."

"Because heaven is a distraction. It's something we talk about when death is theoretical. When it's actually happening, people care about what they're leaving behind, not where they're going."

I met a woman named Grace. Forty-seven. Breast cancer. Two months to live. She told me she had spent the last year trying to figure out what she believed and finally gave up.

"I thought dying would clarify things. Like you get close to the edge and suddenly you know. But it's the opposite. The closer I get, the less certain I am about anything. And you know what? That's okay. I don't need to know. I just need to get through this without falling apart, and I need my kids to be okay."

I asked what she told people when they asked whether she believed in heaven.

"I tell them what they need to hear. If it's my evangelical sister, I say I'm at peace with Jesus. If it's my atheist brother, I say I'm not afraid because I've made peace with mortality. If it's my kids, I tell them I'll always love them. All of those things are true in their own way. Or true enough."

"True enough?"

She smiled, tired but genuine. "Yeah. True enough to help people who love me get through losing me. That's all I can give them. The actual truth about what happens after I die? I'll find out soon enough. Until then, everyone gets the version that helps them most."

After three months at the edge with people who were dying, I understood something I had not expected.

The question people asked was not, "What happens after death?"

The question was, "Will the people I love be okay?"

And the answer they needed was not metaphysical certainty.

It was permission. Permission to hope without knowing. Permission to say, "I don't know, but here's what helps me."

Robert did not need a mansion in heaven. He needed rest.

Helen did not need atheist certainty. She needed to be surprised by the possibility.

Grace did not need truth. She needed to comfort the people she was leaving behind.

At the edge, where death was actually happening, all the theological certainty I had been collecting felt beside the point.

What mattered was comfort. Connection. Permission to not know.

What mattered was being able to say, "I hope there's something," without having to prove it.

Christians like Robert were supposed to be certain about streets of gold, but at two in the morning, they just wanted rest. Atheists like Helen were supposed to be confident about annihilation, but days before death they were open to surprise. And people like Grace were simply making it up as they went along, offering different versions depending on what would help the people they loved most.

Which meant either the traditions had failed to communicate their teachings, or people were customizing heaven regardless of what they had been taught.

Or both.

I needed to understand the gap between what religions actually teach about heaven and what people believe when it matters.

So I started with the tradition that made heaven central to its entire project.

PART II:
HEAVEN WITH RULES

Chapter 5

Heaven With Rules

I attended a Bible study at an evangelical church in Wheaton on a Wednesday night.

Twenty-three people sat in a circle in the basement. Coffee and cookies rested on a table in the corner. Everyone held Bibles filled with highlighted verses and Post-it notes marking favorite passages.

The topic that night was heaven.

The group leader, a man named Greg, asked everyone to describe what they believed heaven would be like.

The answers came quickly.

"We will be reunited with loved ones."

"We will worship God forever."

"There will be no more pain or suffering."

"We will have glorified bodies."

"Jesus will be there, and we will finally see him face to face."

Heads nodded. No one disagreed.

Then Greg asked a follow-up question.

"Does anyone ever have doubts about any of this?"

Silence.

People looked at their Bibles. At their coffee cups. At the floor.

Finally, a woman in her early sixties raised her hand halfway.

"Sometimes I wonder if it's all real. What if we made it up because we can't handle the idea of death being the end?"

The room stayed quiet for a moment.

Then Greg smiled.

"That's a normal question. Satan uses doubt to weaken faith. But we have to remember what Scripture promises. God does not lie. If the Bible says heaven is real, then it is real."

The woman nodded and lowered her hand.

No one else spoke.

After the class ended, I followed her to her car. I introduced myself, explained what I was working on, and asked whether she would be willing to talk privately.

She agreed.

Her name was Linda. She had been attending that church for twenty-three years.

We sat in her car in the parking lot, and I asked her what she actually believed.

"Honestly? I want to believe in heaven. I want to think my husband is somewhere waiting for me. But I also think it might just be a story we tell ourselves so dying feels less frightening."

"Why didn't you say that in class?"

"Because they would think something is wrong with my faith. Or they would try to fix me. Or they would worry about me. It's easier to say what everyone expects."

"Do you think others in the group feel the same way?"

"Probably. But we all say what Christians are supposed to say."

I interviewed a youth pastor named Kyle at a megachurch in Schaumburg. He was thirty-two. He had a theology degree and led a youth group of nearly eighty high school students. He preached about heaven regularly.

I asked him whether he was certain heaven existed.

He glanced around to make sure no one else was nearby.

"Can this be off the record?"

"Yes."

"No. I'm not certain. I hope it's real. I want it to be real. But

I can't say that I know."

"But you teach kids that it is real."

"Because that's my job. And because even if I'm not certain, I think the belief helps them. It gives them hope. It helps them make sense of death. Whether it's literally true or not, it functions as truth in their lives."

"Does that feel dishonest?"

He paused.

"Sometimes. But I also think doubt is part of faith. I'm not lying to them. I'm giving them the tradition I was given, the language I was taught, and trusting they will figure out what they believe as they get older."

"What if they ask you directly whether you believe it?"

"I tell them yes."

"Even though you're not sure?"

"Even though. Because the alternative is telling a sixteen-year-old that I don't know whether their grandmother is anywhere, or whether death is simply the end. That doesn't help anyone."

I met a woman named Deborah at a coffee shop in Glen Ellyn. She was fifty-four, a lifelong Christian who had taught Sunday school for fifteen years.

She told me she stopped believing in heaven three years earlier.

"What changed?"

"My daughter died. Car accident. She was nineteen."

"I'm sorry."

"Everyone at church told me she was in heaven. That she was with Jesus. That I would see her again. And I wanted to believe that. I needed to believe it."

She stirred her coffee slowly.

"But then I started thinking about it seriously. What does it mean to say she's in heaven? Is she nineteen forever? Does she age? Does she have a body? Can she see me? Does she know how much I'm grieving? And if she can see that, how could she be happy? How would that be heaven for her, watching her mother fall apart?"

"What did you conclude?"

"That either heaven doesn't make sense, or it doesn't exist. And the more I thought about it, the more it felt like a story we tell so we don't have to face the reality that she's just gone."

"Do people at your church know you think this?"

"No. I still go every Sunday. I still teach Sunday school. I just don't talk about heaven anymore. If someone asks, I redirect.

Or I quote Scripture and let them assume I believe it."

"Why keep going?"

"Because it's my community. These people love me. They brought meals when my daughter died. They sat with me. They cried with me. I'm not going to take away their faith just because I lost mine."

She paused.

"And honestly, I don't have anywhere else to go."

The pattern appeared everywhere.

Christians were expected to be certain. Certainty was treated as proof of faith. Doubt was framed as weakness, sin, or immaturity.

So people said the right words at the right moments. They nodded during sermons. They affirmed doctrines they privately questioned.

And they kept their doubts hidden because the cost of admitting uncertainty felt too high.

But not everyone was pretending.

I met genuine believers as well. People who had cultivated certainty through decades of prayer and practice. People who spoke about heaven with calm conviction and did not waver even when I pressed them.

I met Rachel at a grief support group at a large evangelical church in Rolling Meadows. She was forty-six, a high school English teacher, and a mother of three. Her middle son, Daniel, had died from leukemia two years earlier. He was fifteen.

When I asked about heaven, she did not hesitate.

"Daniel is there. I know it as surely as I know I'm sitting here talking to you."

"How do you know?"

"Because Jesus promised. John 14:2. 'In my Father's house are many rooms. If it were not so, would I have told you that I go to prepare a place for you?' That's not poetry. That's a promise. And Jesus doesn't lie."

I asked whether she had ever doubted it, especially during Daniel's illness.

"Every single day during treatment," she said. "Especially the bad days. When he was throwing up from chemo, when he couldn't get out of bed, when the pain was so bad he couldn't speak. I would go into the hospital bathroom and scream at God. Ask Him why. Beg Him to heal my son. Tell Him it wasn't fair."

"What answer did you get?"

"No answer. Just this overwhelming sense that Daniel was going to be okay. Not healed. Not cured. But okay. And three days before he died, Daniel told me he had seen Jesus in his room. He said Jesus sat on the edge of his bed and told him not to be afraid."

She stopped to compose herself.

"My husband thought it was the morphine. The hospice nurse said dying patients often hallucinate. But Daniel was calm when he told me. More peaceful than he had been in months. He said, 'Mom, I'm going somewhere better. Don't be sad.'"

"Do you think he really saw Jesus?"

"Yes. Because Daniel changed after that. The fear left. He stopped fighting. He spent his last two days telling me and his dad and his brothers that he loved us, that he would see us again, that we shouldn't worry about him. A fifteen-year-old boy facing death shouldn't have that kind of peace. That came from somewhere else."

I asked how that certainty had helped her.

"It's the only reason I'm still functioning. When I wake up at three in the morning and his room is empty, when I see other kids his age at the grocery store, when his birthday comes around and there's no one to celebrate, the certainty that he's with Jesus is what keeps me from falling apart completely. People tell me I'm using religion as a crutch. Maybe I am. But that crutch is holding me up."

She leaned forward.

"Here's what I know. I prayed for healing and didn't get it.

I prayed for a miracle and watched my son die anyway. If I were making up a comforting story, I would have made up one where God saved him. But I didn't get that story. What I got was the certainty that death isn't the end. That Daniel is somewhere safe. That this separation is temporary. I can't prove it to you. But I've lived it, and it's real."

I met Dorothy at a Catholic church in Wilmette. She was eighty-seven. She had buried three children and her husband.

I asked her whether she believed she would see them again.

"I know I will."

"How do you know?"

"Because God promised. And God keeps His promises."

"But how do you know God's promises are real?"

She smiled, patient with my skepticism in a way that suggested she had heard it before.

"Because I have lived long enough to see Him keep them. When my first son died, I thought I would die from grief. I prayed for strength I did not have, and strength came. Not from me. From somewhere else. When my daughter died, the same thing happened. And when my second son died, and then my husband, the same thing. Each time, I received what I needed exactly when I needed it. That is not chance. That is presence."

"Could it be resilience? Your own psychological strength?"

"It could be. But I know myself. I know my limits. And what I received in those moments was beyond my limits. It came from outside me. And if God was present with me in grief, then He will be present with me in death. If He is present in death, then my children and my husband are with Him. And I will be too."

She folded her hands in her lap.

"After my husband died, I was angry for months. Not at God, but at the unfairness of it all. I had done everything right. I had been faithful. I had raised my children in the Church. And still I lost them, one by one. I demanded answers. I demanded God explain Himself."

"What answer did you get?"

"None. No voice. No vision. No sudden clarity. But I did receive peace. Not all at once. Slowly. Like water seeping into dry ground. I would wake up one morning and realize I had slept through the night. Then a week later I would find myself humming while making coffee. Small things, but unmistakable."

"How did you know it was God and not just time healing?"

"Because time alone doesn't heal grief like that. It softens it, yes. But what I experienced was different. It felt as though someone was carrying me through it. Someone I couldn't see but could feel. And one morning I woke up and knew, not believed but knew, that my children were not gone. They were somewhere. And wherever they were, they were okay. And I would see them again."

"Do you ever doubt?"

"No. Not anymore. I did when I was younger. I had years of wondering whether any of it was real. But after everything I have lived through, doubt feels like a luxury I no longer have access to. I have felt God's presence too many times. I have been carried through too much."

She looked at me gently.

"I can't explain it to someone who hasn't experienced it. But for me, it's as real as the chair I'm sitting in."

I stayed with Dorothy for more than an hour. She told me about her husband, about each of her children, about the ways she believed she would recognize them again. She spoke with a certainty that could not be argued with because it was not built on argument. It was built on experience she could not transfer to me.

She was not performing.

She was not trying to convince me.

She simply believed.

When I asked whether she understood why others doubted, she nodded.

"Of course. I doubted for years. Doubt is not a failure of faith. It is the honest acknowledgment that we do not control when or how God reveals Himself. Some people wait their whole lives and never experience what I have experienced. I don't think that's their fault. I think it's a mystery."

I also spoke with a hospice chaplain named Richard who had worked with dying patients for twenty-six years. He told me he had witnessed the presence of God repeatedly in his work. A peace that descended on terrified patients after prayer. Moments of timing that felt too precise to be a coincidence. Grace that could not be explained by medicine or psychology alone.

"I used to think my faith was something I chose" he said. "After two decades of this work, it feels different. My faith feels given to me through experience. Through repeated encounters with something I cannot explain, but also cannot deny."

These people were not performing certainty.

They had experienced something that made heaven real to them in a way that argument could not reach.

I could not access that experience. I could only document it.

And as I listened, I began to recognize the difference.

Performed certainty sounded defensive and fragile. It needed protection.

Genuine certainty sounded peaceful. It did not need defending.

The problem was that many churches demanded certainty without teaching people how to cultivate it.

They taught doctrine. They taught Scripture. They taught theology.

But they did not teach the practices that might lead to experiential faith. Or if they did, those practices worked for some people and not for others, and no one wanted to say that out loud.

The result was congregations full of people who knew what they were supposed to believe, but did not know how to believe it.

So they pretended together.

A collective agreement where doubt was shameful and certainty was performed.

I interviewed a pastor named Mark who had led a church in Naperville for eighteen years.

He told me something I did not expect.

"About half my congregation doesn't really believe what I preach. Maybe more."

"How do you know?"

"Because I talk to them. In private. At hospital beds. At

funerals. When someone is dying or grieving, the mask comes off. And what I hear isn't certainty. It's hope. People are hoping I'm right, not convinced that I am."

"Does that bother you?"

"It used to. I thought my job was to convince people. To make them certain. But I've come to believe certainty can't be argued into existence. You can offer language, community, and hope, and then trust God to do the rest."

"So you're comfortable with doubt?"

"I would rather people doubt honestly than pretend to believe. But church culture makes that difficult. We built a system where doubt is shameful, so people hide it. And that hiding becomes its own kind of lie."

What I learned from these conversations was this.

For many people, stated belief and actual belief live in separate spaces.

You say you believe in heaven because that is what Christians say.

You participate in the rituals because that is how belonging works.

You repeat the creeds because that is the cost of community.

Privately, you wonder. You doubt. You construct a version of heaven that makes sense to you, even when it contradicts what your church teaches.

And you never say it out loud, because admitting uncertainty feels like failure.

Like you are the only one who has not figured it out yet.

But you are not the only one.

Almost everyone is improvising.

They have simply learned to hide it better.

Chapter 6
The Certainty Problem

Imam Rashid met me at a mosque in Skokie on a Friday afternoon, just after Jummah prayer. The building was modern, constructed within the last decade, with clean lines and a prayer hall large enough to hold three hundred people. We sat in his office, decorated with Arabic calligraphy, shelves of Islamic texts, and a digital clock displaying prayer times. He offered me tea that was aggressively sweet.

I asked him to explain the Islamic view of heaven.

He smiled. "That's easy. We have more details than anyone."

This was not the response I had heard from Christians. They often hesitated, qualified, or admitted uncertainty. Imam Rashid spoke as if the matter were settled doctrine, not open to interpretation.

"The Quran is explicit," he said. "Jannah is paradise. Gardens with rivers. Trees bearing fruit. Peace. No pain, no suffering, no death. You are reunited with loved ones. There are different levels, seven according to most scholars, each more beautiful than the last. And it is eternal. Once you are there, you are there forever."

"And hell?" I asked.

His expression shifted slightly.

"Jahannam. Also real. Also eternal. For those who reject Allah and His messenger, and for those who do evil without repentance. The Quran describes it clearly. Fire. Torment. Separation from Allah's mercy."

"Do you believe that?" I asked. "Eternal hell?"

He paused, choosing his words carefully.

"I believe what the Quran teaches. Allah is the Most Merciful, but He is also the Most Just. Hell is justice for those who knowingly reject truth and cause harm."

"But eternal torment," I said. "Forever?"

Another pause, longer this time.

"The Quran is clear. Scholars have debated what eternity means, whether it is truly without end or simply an unimaginably long time. Some say even hell is ultimately purifying, that Allah's mercy is infinite. Others say eternal means eternal. The texts can support both readings."

"What do you believe?"

"I believe Allah knows better than I do. My role is to teach what is revealed, not to speculate beyond it."

After that conversation, I began speaking with more Muslims. Families, students, professionals, people raised in the faith and converts who had chosen it as adults.

What I found was both fascinating and troubling.

Nearly everyone could recite the official doctrine with precision. Jannah. Jahannam. The Day of Judgment. The scales weigh deeds. The bridge over hell. The intercession of the Prophet. They knew the details better than many Christians knew their own tradition.

But when I asked what they actually believed, when I pressed past the first answers, something else emerged.

I met a woman named Amina, forty-two, Pakistani American, born and raised in Chicago. Her father had died six months earlier from a sudden heart attack.

"What do you believe happened to him?" I asked.

"He is in Jannah. Inshallah," she said. God willing.

"You are certain?"

"He was a good man. He prayed five times a day. He gave to charity. He fasted. He went on Hajj. He lived according to Islam. Why would he not be in Jannah?"

"What if he had doubts? What if he was not perfect?"

She shifted in her seat.

"Everyone makes mistakes. That is why we ask for forgiveness. Allah is merciful."

"But the Quran also speaks about judgment. About hell. Does that worry you?"

She was quiet for a long moment.

"I do not like to think about it," she said finally. "I choose to focus on Allah's mercy, not His wrath. My father was good. I have to believe he is at peace."

"Have to believe?"

She caught herself.

"I do believe," she said. "I just do not like thinking about the alternative."

That was the first crack I noticed in the certainty I had been hearing.

The generational divide was striking.

Older Muslims, especially immigrants, spoke about paradise and hell with confidence. The Quran said it, and that settled it. You lived accordingly or faced the consequences.

Younger American Muslims were far more conflicted.

I met Omar, twenty-four, born in the United States to Egyptian parents. He prayed regularly, fasted during Ramadan, did not drink, and took his faith seriously. But he struggled with its theology.

"I believe in God," he said. "I believe the Quran is a revelation. But the hell part, I cannot reconcile it with a God who is supposed to be more merciful than a mother to her child."

"What does your imam say when you ask?"

"He says I am letting Western values corrupt my understanding of Islam. That mercy does not mean no consequences. That Allah's justice requires hell for those who reject Him. But it doesn't make sense to me."

He shook his head.

"You're telling me someone who lived a good life, helped people, was kind, but did not believe in Islam gets eternal torment? That doesn't feel like mercy. It doesn't feel like justice. It feels tribal."

"Does that make you doubt Islam?"

"It makes me doubt certain interpretations of Islam," he said. "I think we inherited very literal, very harsh readings from medieval scholars who lived in different times. I think Allah's mercy has to be bigger than that."

"Do you talk about this with your family?"

He laughed, without humor.

"No. They already think I'm too American. If I told them I don't believe in eternal hell, they would think I had left Islam."

The question of hell kept resurfacing.

Among Christians, I had encountered a wide range of views. Some believed hell was eternal. Some believed it was temporary. Some believed it was empty. Some believed it was a metaphor.

And all of them were still considered Christian.

In Islam, the space felt narrower.

The Quran speaks about hell repeatedly and vividly. Fire. Boiling water. Skin burned and renewed so suffering continues.

For Muslims who struggled with eternal punishment, there were fewer theological exits.

I met Layla, thirty-one, a convert to Islam. Raised Catholic, she converted in her twenties and was deeply committed to her faith. Yet hell troubled her constantly.

"I fell in love with tawhid," she told me. "With the idea of God's oneness. With prayer. With the discipline. With Islam's emphasis on justice. But Jahannam is the hardest part. The descriptions are terrifying. And it's eternal. Forever. For people who do not believe, even if they were good."

"How do you reconcile that?"

"Some days I tell myself Allah's wisdom is beyond my understanding, and I just need to accept what is revealed. Other days I think maybe the scholars got it wrong. Maybe eternity means something else. Maybe mercy is larger than the literal reading allows."

"Which do you believe?"

She looked exhausted.

"Depends on the day. Depends on whether I'm trying to be a good Muslim or trying to stay sane."

Not everyone struggled.

I met Aisha at a halal restaurant in Naperville. She was thirty-seven, a pediatric oncologist at Lurie Children's Hospital, raised in a Jordanian family but born in the United States. She wore a hijab and prayed in the hospital chapel between rounds. Her daughter Maryam had survived leukemia at age seven. She was now twelve.

"Do you believe your prayers helped save her?" I asked.

"I believe Allah answered them in His way," she said. "I prayed for healing. She got treatment. She survived. Was that Allah working through medicine? Yes. I believe so."

“What if she hadn’t survived? Would you still believe?”

She did not hesitate.

“Yes. Because Allah’s mercy isn’t contingent on getting what I want. It’s trusting that whatever happens is part of His plan, even when I don’t understand it.”

I asked about Jannah. About whether she believed she would see her daughter there someday.

“Absolutely. The Prophet, peace be upon him, said parents who lose young children are reunited with them in paradise. And even if Maryam lives to be ninety, we will be together again. That’s not hope. That’s certainty.”

“How can you be certain?”

“Because Allah promises it. And Allah does not break promises.”

I asked about hell. About whether eternal punishment troubled her.

“It used to,” she said. “In college, studying biology and evolution, hell felt medieval. Barbaric, even. But the more I learned about justice, about consequences, about how actions ripple through the world, the more it made sense.”

“Eternal punishment makes sense?”

"Eternal accountability makes sense," she said. "If our choices matter, then consequences must exist. Mercy without justice isn't mercy. It's indifference."

"But forever?"

"I don't know exactly how mercy and justice meet in eternity," she said. "The Quran gives us the framework. Allah knows the details. That is enough for me."

I met Fatima at a community center in Bridgeview. She was sixty-eight, had immigrated from Egypt in her twenties, raised four children, and buried her husband two years earlier.

"Of course I will see him again," she said. "He is in Jannah, waiting for me."

"Do you ever doubt?"

She shook her head.

"I have lived seventy years. I have seen too much to doubt."

She told me about praying beside her husband as he died.

"Peace filled the room," she said. "Not medicine. Peace. And I knew he was going somewhere."

When I later told Imam Rashid about the doubts I had heard from younger Muslims, he listened quietly.

"Discomfort is a test," he said finally. "Faith is not choosing what feels good. Islam is submission, even when we do not understand."

"But what if that drives people away?" I asked.

He was silent for a long time.

"Then perhaps their faith was weak to begin with."

I left thinking about what certainty costs.

Christians often traded certainty for flexibility. Muslims retained certainty but at the price of moral tension for some believers.

For people like Fatima, certainty was peace.

For people like Omar and Layla, it was weight.

Certainty was meant to comfort.

Sometimes it did.

Sometimes it created a different kind of fear.

Not the fear of not knowing.

But the fear of knowing too much.

Chapter 7

Heaven As Release

I met Priya at a yoga studio in Lincoln Park, which felt appropriate given that we were about to discuss Hindu ideas about the afterlife while sitting on meditation cushions, surrounded by people in expensive athleisure doing downward dog.

Priya was forty-one. She was born in Mumbai, raised in New Jersey, and now lived in Chicago, where she taught comparative religion at DePaul. She agreed to meet after a mutual friend mentioned my project, though she warned me that explaining Hindu views of the afterlife to a Westerner was like trying to explain jazz to someone who had only ever heard marching bands.

“It isn’t that you can’t understand it,” she said. “It’s that your framework for understanding will fight you the whole way.”

She was right. I just did not know yet how viscerally right, how much the conversation ahead would threaten what I thought I wanted from an afterlife.

When I asked her to explain the Hindu view of heaven, she stopped me.

“There isn’t a Hindu view. Hinduism isn’t a single religion

with a single doctrine. It's more like a family of related traditions. They share some texts and concepts, but they diverge wildly on specifics. Some Hindus believe in reincarnation. Some focus on moksha, liberation from the cycle of rebirth. Some believe in multiple heavens and hells. Some treat all of it as a metaphor. It depends on the tradition, the text, the teacher, the region, the century."

"Okay," I said. "So what do you believe?"

She smiled. "That's the better question. I believe in karma and reincarnation. I believe consciousness continues after death, but not in the way most Westerners think. And I believe the goal isn't to go to heaven. The goal is to stop needing to go anywhere."

"Explain that."

She settled deeper into her cushion and, over the next hour, laid out a cosmology so different from the Christian model that I kept stopping her to make sure I was following.

In her tradition, death was a transition. Karma shaped what came next. If your karma was positive, you might be reborn into better circumstances. If it were negative, you might be reborn into a harder life, with sharper consequences and more opportunity to learn.

"So reincarnation is like cosmic education?"

“Sort of,” she said. “It’s a continuation. Consciousness keeps moving until it learns what it needs to learn, until it releases its attachments, until it recognizes its true nature.”

“Which is what?”

“That the individual self is an illusion,” she said. “What you think of as you is a temporary configuration of awareness that believes it’s separate, but it isn’t. The goal is to realize you aren’t a separate wave. You’re the ocean. When you truly know that, you’re liberated. You don’t need to be reborn anymore.”

“Free to do what?”

She shook her head. “That question stops making sense. You’re not a separate thing that needs to do something. You’re just aware, present, one with Brahman, ultimate reality.”

I sat there trying to process it and felt something cold settle in my chest.

Because what Priya was describing as liberation, as the highest achievement of spiritual practice, sounded to me like death. Not symbolic death. Not transformation. The end of everything I thought of as me.

And I realized I was terrified.

“So heaven isn’t the goal,” I said. “The goal is to stop existing as an individual.”

"The goal is to stop thinking you're an individual," she corrected. "You don't stop existing. You realize you were never separate to begin with. What you thought was 'you' was a temporary illusion. Liberation is waking up from that dream."

"That sounds terrifying."

She laughed. "Only if you're attached to being a separate self. If you see separateness as the source of suffering, then the dissolution of the self isn't death. It's freedom."

But I was attached to being a separate self.

I liked being Shehzad. I liked having memories that were mine, relationships that were mine, preferences and quirks, and the particular way I thought that made me distinct from other people.

The idea that all of that was an illusion, that liberation meant dissolving into an undifferentiated cosmic consciousness where there was no more Shehzad, no more individual experience, only awareness without a subject, felt worse than annihilation.

At least annihilation was honest about being the end. This felt like trying to sell the end as enlightenment.

The more I spoke with Hindus and Buddhists, the more I realized how fundamentally different their framework was from the Western heaven model. And the more uncomfortable I became with what that discomfort revealed about me.

Christians, Muslims, Jews, and even most atheists I had spoken to, operated from the same basic assumption: the self is real, continuous, and worth preserving. Heaven is where the self goes and continues, just under better conditions.

In Hindu and Buddhist traditions, the self is the problem.

The self is what suffers. The self is what craves. The self is what fears death.

And the solution is not to preserve the self in a better location. The solution is to recognize that the self was never what it claimed to be.

I met a Buddhist monk named Tenzin at a meditation center in Evanston. He was American, born in Ohio, and ordained for fifteen years. He spoke about death and rebirth with the same casual tone most people use to discuss their commute, which left me both fascinated and unsettled by his comfort with ideas that made my skin crawl.

"In Tibetan Buddhism, we have detailed descriptions of what happens after death," he told me. "The Bardo Thodol, the Tibetan Book of the Dead, maps out the process. Consciousness leaves the body. There are visions, lights, peaceful and wrathful deities. Eventually, you're drawn into rebirth based on karma."

"Do you believe that literally?"

"I believe consciousness continues," he said. "Whether all those details are literal or symbolic, I don't know. But I've been present at enough deaths to know something happens. The body dies, yet there's a process that the body doesn't explain. Something is leaving, even if we don't have instruments to measure it."

I asked whether he was afraid of death.

"No. I'm curious about it. I've been practicing for this my whole monastic life. Meditation is rehearsal for dying. You learn to let go of attachment. You learn to observe consciousness without identifying with it. You learn to be present without clinging. If the practice works, death is like falling asleep consciously. A transition."

"What if you're wrong? What if there's nothing after?"

He shrugged. "Then I lived a good life practicing compassion and awareness. And I won't be around to regret being wrong."

His calmness forced me to see how tightly I had been clinging to the idea of personal continuation, and I did not like what that revealed.

Because what I wanted, what I desperately wanted even though I had avoided admitting it through most of this project, was heaven in the most selfish sense.

I wanted Shehzad to continue. I wanted my memories, my relationships, my specific identity to persist. I wanted to see Margaret again and have her recognize me, to have her know I wrote this book, to watch her give that wry consultant smile.

I wanted reunion, recognition, continuity.

And Eastern traditions were telling me that wanting any of that was the attachment that needed to be released. That clinging to Shehzad was the source of suffering. That the goal was to let Shehzad dissolve into something larger.

And I could not do it.

I could not even pretend I wanted to.

The idea of losing myself, even if I gained cosmic awareness in exchange, felt like a terrible bargain.

Which meant I was either spiritually immature by Eastern standards, or the Eastern goal was death with better marketing, or both.

What fascinated me was how differently Eastern and Western traditions treated the self, and how my resistance to the Eastern view exposed what I was really asking for when I asked about heaven.

Western traditions assume the self is the point. The question is whether the "I" continues. Whether the person I am persists after death.

Eastern traditions respond: you're asking the wrong question.

The "I" you want to preserve is already unstable. You are a temporary pattern in consciousness. When you die, the pattern dissolves, but the ocean remains.

I found this philosophically compelling and emotionally unacceptable. I liked being a self. I liked continuity and memory and relationship.

Dissolution as liberation felt like death with extra steps.

I said as much to Tenzin.

He nodded. "That is the Western mind resisting. You're attached to being Shehzad. And that attachment creates suffering. As long as you believe Shehzad is real and must be protected, you will fear anything that threatens Shehzad's existence. But if you see Shehzad as a story, a useful convention, then death stops being a threat. It becomes the end of one story, and the possibility of other stories, or no stories, or all stories. Whatever comes is okay because you're not clinging to this one."

"But I like this story."

"Of course you do," he said. "It's yours. You've invested decades in it. But liking it doesn't make it permanent. The question is whether you can love the story without needing it to last forever."

I did not have an answer. I only knew the answer was no.

I could not love the story without needing it to last. I could not accept Shehzad as a temporary pattern. I could not embrace dissolution as freedom.

Which meant either I was too immature to understand enlightenment, or enlightenment was a way of making peace with annihilation by reframing it as transcendence. And I was not ready to make that peace.

The American adaptation of Eastern spirituality was even more confusing, and in some ways more disturbing, because it revealed how badly we want to keep the self while claiming to transcend it.

I met people who called themselves Buddhist but talked about reincarnation as a way to preserve personal identity. "I think I was Cleopatra in a past life," one woman told me at a spiritual center in Naperville. "I have these memories, these feelings of familiarity when I read about ancient Egypt."

That was the opposite of what Buddhism taught.

Buddhism says there is no permanent self to reincarnate. What continues is karma, consequence, pattern, but not personal identity. You do not come back as you.

Yet American spirituality had taken reincarnation and turned it into a way to preserve the self across lifetimes, which was precisely what the original teaching was trying to dismantle.

"When I die," one yoga teacher told me, "my consciousness will return to universal consciousness. But I'll still be me, expanded. I'll see all my past lives, understand all the lessons, and then choose whether to reincarnate again or stay in higher dimensions."

"Where did you learn that?" I asked.

"I just know it," she said. "It feels right."

It was theology by vibes. She had taken moksha, non-self, and New Age language and assembled a personalized afterlife that preserved individual identity while claiming Eastern wisdom.

But it made her happy.

And who was I to tell her she was wrong when I was doing the same thing, just with more anxiety.

I wanted heaven to preserve Shehzad. She wanted universal consciousness to preserve her expanded self. We were both clinging to continuation, just with different vocabulary.

I spent three months talking to Hindus, Buddhists, and American practitioners of Eastern-influenced spirituality, and what I discovered was not only what they believed about the afterlife.

I discovered my own terror of nonexistence, and how that

terror had been driving every question I had asked since Margaret died.

I did not want to know what happens after death. I wanted someone to promise me that I would not end. That Shehzad would continue. That death would not be the final separation from everyone I loved.

Eastern traditions were telling me that wanting that was the problem. That clinging to Shehzad was what made death terrifying. That liberation meant letting go of exactly what I was trying to preserve.

And I could not do it.

I could not let go of Shehzad. I could not embrace dissolution. I could not reframe annihilation as enlightenment.

Which made me wonder whether heaven was ever about truth or enlightenment or cosmic awareness.

Maybe heaven was about humans refusing to accept that we end. Maybe it was an elaborate structure built to avoid facing impermanence. And maybe Eastern traditions were honest enough to say the quiet part out loud: the self you are trying to save was never as solid as you think.

But if the self was not solid, then what was I?

What was this thing experiencing terror at the thought of

dissolution? What was this consciousness clinging so desperately to continuation?

I did not know.

What I did know was that I would rather cling to the illusion of Shehzad than accept transcendence if transcendence required losing everything I thought of as me. I would rather be spiritually immature than cosmically aware if awareness meant I could not remain myself.

Maybe that made me exactly the kind of attached, suffering being Eastern traditions were trying to help.

Or maybe it made me honest.

Honest that I valued individual existence over transcendence. Honest that I would take limited consciousness over unlimited awareness if it meant I could stay Shehzad.

The question was whether heaven was possible without that bargain. Whether there was a framework in which Shehzad could continue without dissolving into the ocean. Where love could persist without the self disappearing. Where death did not require either eternal separation or cosmic merger, but something else entirely.

I did not know whether that framework existed.

But I knew I needed to look for it.

Chapter 8

The Jewish Shrug

Rabbi Cohen met me at a deli in Skokie, which felt thematically perfect for a conversation about Jewish perspectives on the afterlife. We ordered pastrami sandwiches large enough to feed small families, and before I asked my first question, he said, "You know we don't really focus on this, right?"

"On what?"

"Heaven. The afterlife. What happens when you die. It's not really our thing."

I had heard versions of that line before, but I wanted to understand it more clearly. If I am being honest, I also wanted to understand why the idea of not focusing on it made me so uneasy.

Every Jewish person I mentioned the project to responded the same way: we don't worry about that; we focus on this life; the afterlife is beside the point.

It fascinated me because Judaism sits at the foundation of Christianity and Islam, both of which are consumed by the afterlife. Somewhere between the Torah and the New Testament, heaven became the main event.

But Judaism itself seemed remarkably unconcerned. That unconcern exposed something in me. Not just curiosity, but hunger. A desperate need for certainty I had been trying not to name.

"So what do you believe happens after death?" I asked.

Rabbi Cohen took a bite, chewed slowly, and said, "I have no idea."

"No ideas at all?"

"I have ideas," he said. "The tradition has ideas. We have Sheol, the place of the dead. We have Gan Eden, paradise. We have Gehenna, which is a temporary purification, not eternal hell. We have resurrection of the dead in the messianic age. We have Olam Ha-Ba, the world to come. We have Maimonides' thirteen principles, including belief in resurrection. We have mystical ideas like gilgul, reincarnation. We have plenty of ideas."

"But you don't know which one is right."

"Nobody knows which one is right," he said. "That's part of it. Judaism is comfortable with not knowing. We're not a religion of creeds. We're a religion of practice. You don't have to believe the right things about heaven to be a good Jew. You have to live ethically. You have to study. You have to keep mitzvot, the commandments. What happens after you die? God will figure that out. Your job is to live well now."

It was so different from the Christian clergy I had spoken with, where heaven sat at the center of the theological project. For Rabbi Cohen, the afterlife was not central. It was almost incidental.

And as he said, "God will figure that out," with the calm of someone stating a basic fact, I felt something twist inside me. Something uncomfortably like jealousy.

Because I wanted that ease. I wanted to be able to shrug and say, live well now, and mean it. I wanted to let go of the need to solve death like a problem. But I could not.

For months I had been collecting beliefs, mapping cosmologies, and interviewing experts. Beneath all of it was the same hope: that someone would give me certainty, that someone would tell me the truth about what happens when we die. Rabbi Cohen was explaining, gently but firmly, that nobody had that truth and Judaism was fine with it.

"But don't people ask?" I said. "Don't congregants want to know what happened to their loved ones?"

"Of course they ask," he said. "And I tell them what the tradition teaches. I also tell them the tradition teaches multiple things, and decent people disagree, and that's okay. The Talmud is full of disagreement. We don't need unanimous certainty about the afterlife. We need commitment to justice, compassion, and study."

Then he added, "And I tell them their loved one is at peace and their memory is a blessing, which is true regardless of your metaphysics."

After that, I started speaking with more Jewish people. Different denominations, different levels of observance, different generations.

What I found was a consistent inconsistency. Nobody had a single clear answer about heaven. Nobody seemed bothered by that.

Most responded to questions about the afterlife with intellectual humility and practical focus. Live well. Do good. Remember the dead. Carry them forward.

And I found myself growing more frustrated, not with them, but with myself. Their comfort with uncertainty made my own discomfort impossible to ignore.

How could they let this go? Why did I need certainty so badly? Why was I spending two years on the question if the healthiest response was apparently to stop asking it?

Sarah, thirty-seven, Reform, told me she had attended synagogue her whole life and could not remember ever hearing a sermon about heaven.

"Our sermons are about the Torah portion, about ethics, about current events, about how to live Jewishly in the modern world. The afterlife just doesn't come up."

"What do you think happens when you die?"

"Honestly, I go back and forth. Sometimes I think there's something. Sometimes I think it's lights out. Sometimes I wonder if there's some kind of continuity, but not the way religions describe it. Mostly, I don't think about it. I have enough to worry about in this life."

"But when someone you love dies, what do you tell yourself?"

She finished her coffee, thinking.

"I tell myself their suffering is over. I tell myself their memory lives in the people who loved them. I tell myself the impact they had continues even though they're gone. Whether there's also an afterlife where they continue as themselves, I hope so. But I don't know. And I'm okay not knowing."

She said it the way someone says, I don't like mushrooms. Not as a spiritual achievement, not as a philosophy. Just: uncertainty is acceptable.

And part of me wanted to shake her. To ask how she could stand it. How could she love people knowing they might end completely and still be okay with not knowing if she would ever see them again.

But I didn't. I nodded, wrote notes, and felt panic rising that maybe the Jewish approach was right. Maybe the healthiest response to the heaven question was to stop demanding an answer.

And that possibility frightened me more than any answer I had heard.

David, sixty-two, Conservative, had lost his wife two years earlier. His rabbi spoke about Olam Ha-Ba, about her neshamah being at peace, about resurrection in the messianic age, about memory and continuity.

"Did any of it help?" I asked.

"Some of it," he said. "The memory part helped. Thinking about how she changed people, how her kindness rippled out, how she made the world different by being in it. That felt real. The heaven part?" He shrugged. "I'm not sure I believe it. But I appreciate that Judaism doesn't require me to believe it with certainty. I can hold it loosely. I can hope it's true without needing to be sure."

I can hold it loosely.

The phrase stayed with me for weeks because it described something I could not do.

I could not hold beliefs loosely. I needed to know whether they were true or false, real or imagined. I wanted conviction or rejection, not this middle ground of hopeful uncertainty that so many Jewish people seemed to inhabit without effort.

And I realized what I envied was not their beliefs about heaven.

It was their freedom from needing those beliefs to be certain.

Josh, twenty-six, identified as Jewish culturally but not religiously.

"What do you think happens when you die?" I asked.

"Probably nothing," he said. "Your brain stops, your consciousness ends, you decompose. That's it."

"Does that scare you?"

"Not really. I'm not excited about it, but it doesn't keep me up at night. I won't be around to experience not existing, so what's there to fear?"

"But what about people you love who die? Do you think they're just gone?"

He hesitated.

"Yeah," he said. "That's harder. When my grandpa died last year, I had this moment where I wanted there to be something after. He was a good person. It felt wrong that someone like that just disappears. But wanting something to be true doesn't make it true.

So I try to remember him. Tell stories. Live in a way that would make him proud. That feels more real than imagining him in an afterlife."

Wanting doesn't make it true.

That was exactly what I had been avoiding throughout this project.

I wanted heaven to be real. I wanted consciousness to continue. I wanted to see Margaret again. I wanted death not to be a final separation.

And I had been collecting beliefs as if enough information would somehow prove that what I wanted was true.

Josh, this twenty-six-year-old secular Jew, said what I had refused to face: wanting does not make it so, and you can survive grief without needing the afterlife to be real.

A pattern emerged across the Jewish conversations, something that felt distinctly Jewish: doubt as a feature, not a flaw.

Christianity often treats doubt as a problem to overcome. Certainty is the goal. Faith becomes something you struggle to hold onto. Doubt becomes something you confess, pray through, and defeat.

Judaism treats doubt as a normal part of intellectual life. The Talmud is built on disagreement. Wrestling with God is embedded in the tradition. Questioning is not merely tolerated. It is expected.

So when it comes to the afterlife, where there is no proof and multiple possible interpretations and no requirement for uniform belief, Judaism shrugs.

Maybe there is heaven. Maybe there isn't. Maybe it's a metaphor. Maybe it's literal. Nobody knows for sure, and pretending to know would be dishonest.

And watching Jewish people live full lives while holding heaven loosely, while focusing on ethics instead of metaphysics, I felt envy so strong it started to resemble grief.

Because what they had was the ability to make peace with not knowing.

And I did not.

I needed certainty. I needed someone to promise me that death was not final, that consciousness continued, that I would see the people I loved again.

Rabbi Goldstein, an elderly Orthodox man in his eighties, had studied Torah his entire life. I asked him what he believed about the afterlife.

"I believe what the tradition teaches," he said. "Resurrection of the dead. The world to come. Reward for the righteous. Punishment for the wicked, though temporary, is because God is merciful."

"But in your heart, do you think that's what actually happens?"

He looked at me for a long moment, then said, "I believe God is just. I believe our lives matter. I believe the righteous do not labor in vain. Beyond that, I have faith, not knowledge. And faith is enough."

"What if you're wrong?"

"Then I lived a good life according to the commandments," he said. "And I'll learn what's true when I die. Either way, I did what I was supposed to do. That's all any of us can control."

There was something almost refreshing about that after months of listening to people perform certainty while privately doubting.

Judaism gave people permission to not know. Permission to focus on what could be done rather than what could not be proved. Permission to say, I hope there's something, but I'm not sure, and that's okay.

And I envied that permission more than I envied any confident description of heaven.

Because certainty, whether it was streets of gold or gardens with rivers, came with costs. It asked people to defend what they could not prove, to speak with confidence they did not always feel, to build elaborate structures to avoid admitting ignorance.

The Jewish shrug did not require any of that. It required honesty about the limits of human knowledge and a decision to live well anyway.

Back at the deli, I asked Rabbi Cohen why Judaism could live with uncertainty about the afterlife when other Abrahamic traditions demanded more clarity.

He thought for a moment while he worked on his pickle.

"I think it's because we've been through so much," he said. "Exile. Diaspora. Persecution. The Holocaust. We've had to keep identity and faith through circumstances that should have destroyed us. You can't do that if your faith depends on a detailed map of what happens after you die. You need something more durable."

"What's more durable?" I asked.

"Practice," he said. "Community. Ethics. Study. The things you can do regardless of metaphysical certainty. I can observe Shabbat whether or not I'm sure about heaven. I can pursue justice whether or not I believe in resurrection. I can study Torah without needing a firm theory of what happens to my soul. The tradition gives me a way to live meaningfully without requiring certainty about the unknowable."

"But doesn't that leave people without comfort?" I asked. "When they're grieving or afraid, don't they want answers?"

"They want comfort," he said. "Answers and comfort aren't the same. I can comfort someone by sitting with them, by helping them say Kaddish, by reminding them their loved one's memory is a blessing, and by connecting them to community and continuity. I don't need a detailed map of the afterlife to do that."

"What do you say when someone asks directly, will I see my husband again?"

He put down his sandwich and looked at me.

"I say this: if there is an afterlife, and if it's anything like what we hope, then yes, you'll see him again. And if there isn't, then his love shaped you, and that shaping continues. Either way, your love was real, your grief is real, and what's real doesn't vanish just because we can't explain where it goes."

"That isn't really an answer," I said.

"No," he agreed. "It isn't. But it's honest. And sometimes honesty is better than false certainty."

After months of speaking with Jewish people across the spectrum, from Orthodox to fully secular, I walked away with something I did not expect: envy.

Not envy of their beliefs about heaven, because most did not hold those beliefs tightly, if they held them at all.

Envy of their comfort with not knowing.

They had built a tradition that did not require certainty about the afterlife. They had found meaning, purpose, community, and ethical direction without needing to solve death.

They had made peace with mystery.

And watching them do it, I started to wonder whether that was the more honest approach, and whether my inability to adopt it revealed something broken in me or something unavoidably human.

Maybe the rest of us were trying too hard to know what cannot be known. Maybe we were building elaborate theological architectures to avoid admitting we were guessing.

Maybe the Jewish shrug, the calm acceptance of "we don't really know, and that's okay," was closer to the truth than any of the detailed heaven maps I had been collecting.

But I wasn't sure I could live there.

I had spent two years searching for certainty, mapping beliefs as if enough information would produce an answer. I kept asking heaven to become something I could understand, when maybe heaven was never meant to be understood. Maybe it could only be hoped for, or released.

And the Jewish tradition kept suggesting the same unsettling possibility: that the healthiest response to the heaven question is to stop demanding certainty and focus on living well.

Because the more people I interviewed, the more obvious it became that nobody knew anything for sure.

Some people simply admitted it more easily. And the ones who admitted it, who said uncertainty is acceptable, seemed to carry more peace than the people who claimed certainty while hiding private doubt.

But I still couldn’t do it.

I still needed someone to promise me that death wasn’t final.

And that need, that clinging to certainty about what cannot be verified, was starting to feel like the real problem I had to face, not the heaven question itself.

Chapter 9

The Man Who Lied To His Family

David was dying in a way that was both ordinary and unbearable, which is probably true of most deaths. Pancreatic cancer, stage four, metastasized to his liver and lungs. The doctors had given him three months. That was six weeks ago.

A friend in the philosophy department at Northwestern connected us. "David wants to talk to you about your project," he said. "He has thoughts, and not much time."

We met in his hospice room on a Thursday afternoon. The room was clean and impersonal in the way hospital rooms are, trying to feel warm and failing. David lay propped on pillows, oxygen cannula in his nose, looking like a man who had been substantial once and was now being slowly erased.

He was seventy-one. A philosophy professor for forty years, specializing in ethics and epistemology. He had written books about moral reasoning and the nature of knowledge. He had spent a career asking what we can know and what we owe each other.

I assumed he wanted to offer some final synthesis, some clean conclusion to a life devoted to thinking.

Instead, he wanted to tell me about lying to his family.

"They were here yesterday," he said. "My daughter brought the grandkids. Three of them. Seven through twelve. They stood around the bed looking terrified, trying not to cry, trying to be brave."

He paused to catch his breath. Even speaking costs him now.

"My daughter asked me if I was at peace. Specifically, she asked: Dad, are you at peace knowing you'll see Mom again?"

His wife had died three years earlier. Breast cancer. They had been married for forty-six years. Her funeral had been at an evangelical church, her church, not his. The pastor had spoken about reunion, eternal life, and death as a doorway.

David had sat through it all in silence.

"What did you tell your daughter?" I asked.

"I told her yes," he said. "I told her I was at peace. I told her I believed I would see her mother again."

He looked at me with eyes that were still sharp, still him, despite everything the cancer was doing.

"I lied."

David had been an atheist since graduate school. Not angry, not performative, not interested in conversion debates. He had examined the arguments and found them unconvincing. He had never hidden it. His family knew. They had spent decades trying to convert him, gently at first, then with increasing urgency as he aged.

His wife had been a believer, serious and committed but not rigid. Their marriage had held the tension with respect and occasional strain. She went to church. He stayed home and read the paper. She prayed for him. He loved her anyway.

When she died, the family gathered around and talked about heaven with absolute confidence. She was with Jesus now. Free. Waiting. They would see her again. David said nothing.

"I didn't see the point in telling them what I actually thought," he said. "That she was gone. That her consciousness ended when her brain stopped. That there was no her anymore, just a body that used to contain her. What would that accomplish, except making their grief harder?"

"So you stayed quiet."

"I stayed quiet. They assumed I agreed, or at least hoped they were right, and I let them assume it. Challenging it then would have been cruel."

He shifted slightly and winced. The pain medication helped, but it could not erase everything.

"But now I'm the one dying," he said. "And they want to

know I'm okay. They want to know I'm not afraid. They want to know I believe I'll see their mother again. If I tell them the truth, that I think death is final and consciousness ends and there's nothing after, they will spend my last weeks trying to save my soul. They'll bring pastors. They'll cry. They'll beg me to accept Jesus. They'll make my death about their fear instead of my peace."

"So you lied."

"I chose comfort over truth," he said. "Not my comfort. Theirs."

I sat there, unsure what to say. In months of interviews, this was the first time someone had admitted, so plainly, to deliberately misrepresenting what they believed about death.

"Does it bother you?" I asked. "Lying about something that fundamental?"

He smiled, a tired smile, like he had been turning this question over for a long time.

"It should bother me," he said. "I've spent my career arguing that honesty is a primary virtue, that we owe each other truth, that lying undermines trust and distorts reality. I've written papers about this. I've taught seminars about this. And now, at the end, I discover I don't actually live that way. Or maybe I believe it in theory but not in practice."

“Or maybe there are different kinds of truth,” I said.

“Maybe,” he said. “Or maybe love is a higher virtue than truth, and I never admitted it because it complicated my philosophy.”

He paused again. Breathing, even with oxygen, had become labor.

“Here’s what I’ve realized,” he said. “Truth matters. Honesty matters. But relationship matters more. Sometimes honesty destroys a relationship without producing any meaningful benefit. My daughter needs to believe her parents will be reunited. My grandchildren need to believe death isn’t a final separation. Telling them I think consciousness ends when the brain stops, that doesn’t give them truth in any useful sense, because nobody actually knows what happens after death. It just takes away comfort and replaces it with nothing but my intellectual consistency. That helps no one.”

“But does that make belief meaningless?” I asked. “If you can just lie when it’s convenient?”

“I’m not lying about belief,” he said. “I’m lying about my belief. There’s a difference. Heaven might be real. I don’t think it is, but I don’t know for certain. And my daughter’s belief is real for her. It shapes how she lives, how she grieves, how she makes sense of loss. Who am I to take that from her? What right do I have to dismantle her entire cosmology so I can die with philosophical consistency?"

We talked for another hour. He got tired quickly, so we paused often, but he kept insisting we continue. He had been thinking about this for weeks and wanted to tell someone who could hold the complexity without trying to fix it.

"Do you feel guilty?" I asked.

"Yes and no," he said. "Yes, because lying violates a principle I've carried my whole life. No, because the alternative would cause more harm. Ethics isn't rigid rule-following. It's navigating competing values and choosing the least damaging option in imperfect circumstances. I prioritized my family's peace over my own consistency. That might fail a strict reading of some ethical theories, but it feels right by the standard of love."

He closed his eyes for a while, not sleeping, just resting.

Then he said, "You know what's funny? For forty years I taught students to question everything, to examine assumptions, to demand evidence, not to believe things just because they're comforting. And now I'm participating in exactly the kind of social performance I spent my career critiquing."

"Does that make you a hypocrite?"

"Maybe," he said. "Or maybe it makes me human. Humans lie constantly to smooth social life, to protect feelings, to preserve community. And sometimes those lies are more ethical than the truth would be."

He opened his eyes and looked directly at me.

"My daughter isn't asking me for a philosophical lecture on consciousness. She's asking me if she's going to lose me forever. The answer she can live with is no, we'll see each other again. The answer she can't live with is yes, I'm gone completely and permanently. So I give her what she can live with. Is that truth or love?"

I left his room shaken in a way I hadn't expected.

I had spent months collecting beliefs about heaven, categorizing what people said they believed, and assuming stated belief was actual belief.

David shattered that assumption.

If he could lie, deliberately, lovingly, about something as central as death, then how much of what I'd gathered was performance?

When someone said, "They're in a better place now," did they believe it, or were they reciting the line?

When a pastor preached about streets of gold, did he believe it, or was he maintaining a tradition because it held the room together?

When people spoke with confidence, were they confident, or were they performing confidence because doubt felt like failure?

I went back to see David once more before he died. His daughter sat beside his bed holding his hand. She talked about his wife, about family vacations, holidays, small domestic moments that sounded, in her telling, like sacred history.

David smiled and nodded and added a detail now and then, just enough to keep the story alive.

She said, “I can’t wait for you two to be reunited. I bet Mom’s getting everything ready for you.”

David squeezed her hand and said, “I’m sure she is.”

His face held nothing but love.

After she left, I asked how he felt about sustaining the pretense.

“Peaceful,” he said. “For the first time in weeks, actually peaceful. I was afraid I’d blurt out the truth in some morphine moment, that I’d fail at this and make it messy. But it turns out it’s easy.”

“Easy?”

“Because it isn’t really lying,” he said. “It’s loving them the way they need to be loved right now.”

"Even if it means dying alone with your actual beliefs?"

"I'm not alone with my beliefs," he said. "I'm alone in my certainty. But so is everyone else. Nobody knows what happens after death. I think it's nothing. My daughter thinks it's heaven. We're both guessing, based on incomplete information and psychological need. The difference is my guess isolates people, and hers connects them. So I'll let her keep hers. And I'll die having given her that gift."

David died two days later, surrounded by family, apparently at peace, apparently certain about reunion with his wife, apparently having found faith at the end.

That is what the obituary said. That is what his family believes.

And I am the only person who knows otherwise.

I thought about David for months. About what it meant that he lied, about whether he was right, about whether I would do the same thing.

And I realized he had exposed the question I'd been avoiding.

It wasn't only, what people believe about heaven.

It was why people need to believe anything at all.

And maybe more importantly, when belief is about truth, and

when it is about survival.

David chose survival. Not his own. His body was dying regardless. He chose his family's ability to grieve without collapsing, his daughter's faith, and his grandchildren's sense that death is not final separation.

He sacrificed intellectual honesty on the altar of their emotional life.

I still don't know whether that was noble or cowardly or simply human.

But it cracked something in me.

I had been trying to map belief as if belief were a stable object, something you could chart and categorize, and understand from what people said.

David showed me that belief is also something people do. Something they perform. Something they adjust based on who is listening and what the moment can bear.

And sometimes belief has nothing to do with truth at all.

Sometimes it is just love.

Love for the people you are leaving behind.

And maybe that is what heaven has always been. Not a place we go when we die, but what love does when it refuses to accept death as final. Not a reward, not a waiting room, not a literal geography.

Just the story we tell when absence is too permanent to hold.

The architecture humans build to keep relationships alive after the body is gone.

Heaven as the place love insists exists, because love cannot accept that everything ends.

Heaven is what happens when love refuses to disappear.

PART III:
WHEN BELIEF BREAKS

Chapter 10

What I No Longer Believe

I did not sleep much the night David died.

I kept seeing his daughter in that hospital hallway. I kept hearing the relief in her voice when she said her father had found faith at the end. She sounded certain he was at peace, certain he was not afraid, certain he would see her mother again. Belief gave her a kind of comfort I could almost feel through the phone line.

And I kept thinking about David in that bed, hours from death, maintaining a fiction because the truth would have helped no one.

At 3 AM I was sitting in my kitchen with coffee and eight months of interview notes spread across the table, and I realized I had been asking the wrong questions this entire time.

I started this project asking: What do people believe about heaven?

I asked it as if belief were simple. As if you could ask a person what they believed and they would give you a stable answer, consistent across days and situations, and that answer would mean what it claimed to mean.

David showed me that belief is not simple at all.

People do not only believe things. They perform belief for social reasons. They adjust what they say based on context and audience. They state beliefs they do not actually hold. They hold beliefs they cannot articulate. They carry contradictions without noticing, or they notice and carry them anyway.

They believe things that comfort them regardless of evidence. They stop believing things once those beliefs stop working.

Belief is not a map of reality. It is a tool for navigating reality.

And I had been cataloging the tools without asking what work they were actually doing.

So I went back through my notes, all two hundred-plus interviews, and I started reading them differently.

I stopped asking, "What does this person believe?" and I started asking, "What is this belief doing for them?"

Once I saw it that way, everything changed.

The woman who told me with absolute certainty that her mother was in heaven watching over her was not primarily making an empirical claim about the location of consciousness after death. She was maintaining connection. She was refusing to accept that death meant total separation. Her belief kept her mother present.

The pastor who preached about streets of gold and mansions and eternal worship was not providing architectural details of the afterlife. He was giving his congregation hope that suffering was not meaningless, that injustice would be corrected, that their difficult lives were building toward something better. His belief made present suffering bearable.

The hospice nurse who told dying patients they would see their loved ones again was not delivering a verified report. She was offering permission to let go. She was giving them something to move toward instead of only something they were losing. Her belief turned terror into transition.

The child who described heaven as a creative mode, where nobody can hurt you, was not building theology. He was building safety. He was inventing a place where harm could not follow you. His belief made death less terrifying.

Most of them were not mainly concerned with whether their belief was true in some objective sense.

They were concerned with whether it worked. Whether it helped. Whether it made life more bearable and death less terrifying and grief more survivable.

This forced me to rethink what I thought I understood about

religious belief.

I had been operating with an assumption I did not even know I was carrying. I assumed people believed in heaven because they thought it was real. I assumed belief was fundamentally about describing what exists. I assumed religion, at its core, was trying to get reality right.

But what if that was not the primary function?

What if belief were less about describing reality and more about surviving reality?

What if heaven was not a claim about the afterlife so much as a claim about the necessity of hope?

What if all these different versions of heaven, contradictory and evolving and personally customized, were not attempts to map a place but attempts to solve the unsolvable problem of mortality?

The problem is simple and impossible. Everyone you love will die. You will die. Human consciousness can say those words and even understand them intellectually, but it struggles to hold their full weight. We cannot really sustain the permanent absence of the people we need.

So we create heaven.

Not because we have evidence for it. Not because scripture is perfectly clear. Not because the theology is coherent.

We create it because we have to.

Because the alternative, sitting with permanent loss and eventual personal annihilation, is psychologically unsustainable for most people.

Heaven is what you build when you cannot accept that death is final.

And maybe that is not a moral failure. Maybe it is a human reflex. Maybe it is how love tries to keep going.

This is where I started to unravel.

Because I had spent months collecting beliefs, and now I was realizing that truth and belief might not be tightly linked. Sometimes they were. Often they were not.

That left me with two possibilities, and I hated both.

Either everyone I talked to was participating in a massive collective delusion, building elaborate fictions to avoid facing reality.

Or truth and usefulness were different categories, and religion was never supposed to be primarily about truth in the first place.

The first option meant billions of people had devoted their lives to a story that was not true. It meant theology and prayer and ritual were sophisticated self-deception. It meant David's lie was simply the last version of the same lie, and maybe it was the most honest thing he could offer.

The second option meant my entire framework for understanding belief was wrong. It meant there might be no clean answer to "what happens after death" because the question itself might be malformed. It meant the point might not be to know, but to live without knowing.

I sat with those options for weeks.

I reread interviews. I followed up with people. I asked different questions. And slowly, reluctantly, I began to accept that I had been wrong about almost everything I thought I would discover.

I had started this project believing that people's stated beliefs reflected their actual beliefs.

I no longer believed that.

What people stated was often a socially acceptable version of a much more complicated internal reality. People performed certainty in public while carrying doubt in private. They used traditional language to describe highly personal cosmologies. They claimed to believe what their tradition taught while quietly believing something else.

I had believed religious people were certain and atheists were certain and everyone had picked a side.

I no longer believed that either.

Almost nobody was actually certain. They performed with certainty because admitting uncertainty felt like failure. Religious people had moments of serious doubt. Atheists had moments of wishful hope. Most people lived somewhere in the middle, believing on some days and doubting on others, and then feeling guilty about the inconsistency.

I had believed belief was primarily about truth claims, about what actually exists.

I no longer believed that.

Belief was primarily about survival. It was about making mortality bearable. It was about maintaining relationships beyond death. It was about finding meaning in suffering. It was about refusing to accept that everything ends. Whether those beliefs corresponded to objective reality often seemed secondary. What mattered was whether they helped people live with less fear and die with less despair.

I had believed heaven was a place people thought they would go.

I no longer believed that, at least not in the way I used to mean it.

Heaven was not only a place. It was a promise.

A promise that love does not end. That separation is not final. That the people we need do not simply vanish. That suffering is not pointless. That death is not the ultimate victor.

Whether that promise was true or not, people needed to believe it was. And maybe that need was more fundamental than the question of proof.

The question I started with was: What do people believe about heaven?

The question I was now asking was: What does heaven allow people to survive?

And that changed everything.

Because once I asked it that way, I stopped judging people's beliefs as coherent or incoherent, sophisticated or naive, true or false. I started asking: What work is this belief doing? What problem is it solving? What would collapse if this person stopped believing it?

The mother who believed her stillborn baby was in heaven was not arguing about infant salvation. She was refusing to accept that her child's brief life ended in nothing but loss. Her belief kept her from falling into despair.

The man dying of ALS who believed heaven meant freedom from his failing body was not outlining doctrine about resurrected flesh. He was trying to protect his dignity. He was insisting his consciousness was larger than his deterioration. His belief let him die without bitterness.

The teenager who believed in reincarnation was not presenting a scholarly position on souls. She was giving herself permission to change. She was imagining a future beyond her worst moments. Her belief made transformation possible.

The old woman who believed her husband was watching over her was not trying to prove the dead have errands. She was maintaining connection with the person who had shaped her entire adult life. Her belief kept her from becoming completely alone.

None of them needed their belief to be true in an empirical sense.

They needed it to be true enough.

True enough to get through the day without falling apart.

True enough to face death without drowning in terror.

True enough to survive grief without giving up entirely.

I realized I had been thinking about belief the way a philosopher thinks about belief, as a proposition that is either true or false, rational or irrational, justified or unjustified.

But most people do not relate to their beliefs that way.

They relate to belief the way you relate to a life raft. You do not ask whether a life raft is philosophically justified. You ask whether it keeps you afloat. You do not care whether it is elegant or consistent with your other beliefs about buoyancy. You care whether it works.

Heaven was a life raft.

And I had been asking people to justify their life raft while they were drowning.

This left me in a strange position.

I entered this project thinking I was mapping territory, collecting data, finding patterns, and building a comprehensive picture of contemporary American beliefs about the afterlife.

But I was not mapping territory.

I was cataloging survival strategies.

And survival strategies cannot be judged as true or false. They can only be judged as helpful or harmful. As life-sustaining or life-destroying.

Which meant the question was not, "Do people believe the right things about heaven?"

The question was, "Do people's beliefs about heaven help them live better and die easier?"

And the answer was complicated.

For some people, belief in heaven did enormous good. It gave comfort in grief. It made suffering bearable. It maintained connection with the dead. It created community. It made death less terrifying.

For other people, belief in heaven did harm. It made them afraid of hell. It created anxiety about whether they were saved. It taught them to judge others as damned. It prevented honest grief. It made them discount this life in favor of the next.

For most people, it did both. Helpful and harmful. Comforting and destabilizing. A shelter and a cage, depending on the day.

I went back and reread my notes from David, the philosopher who lied to his family about believing in heaven.

At first, I had been consumed by the moral question. Was it right to lie? Is honesty always the highest virtue? Can love justify deception?

Now I understood what David had been trying to show me.

He was not asking whether heaven was real.

He was asking what belief did, and what human need it served.

In his particular situation, in his particular family,

maintaining the fiction did more good than exposing his atheism would have done. He chose function over truth.

Not because he thought truth did not matter, but because he believed relationship mattered more.

And maybe that was the most honest thing anyone told me throughout this entire project.

Because everyone else was acting as if belief was about truth when it was often about a relationship. About maintaining a connection. About preserving hope. About surviving loss.

David simply admitted it.

Late one night, a few weeks after his funeral, I wrote in my journal: I no longer know what question I am trying to answer.

I started by asking what people believed.

Then I asked why they believed.

Then I asked what their beliefs were doing.

And now I was asking: What is heaven, really? Not the place, if it exists, but the concept. The need. The human impulse to build something beyond death.

I did not have an answer.

But I had a suspicion.

Heaven is not where people go when they die.

Heaven is what happens when love refuses to accept death as final.

It is the story consciousness tells itself when it cannot process permanent absence.

It is the architecture humans build to hold space for a continued relationship with the dead.

It is the promise that lets people survive loss without collapsing.

Whether that promise is true or not, whether heaven exists or does not exist, started to feel almost beside the point.

What mattered was that humans needed to make it.

And we have been making it, in every culture and every era, in thousands of forms, since the beginning of consciousness.

Not because we had proof.

Because we could not live without hope.

I began this project trying to stay objective, trying to collect data without imposing my own grief on the material.

But David's death changed me.

I was no longer only collecting. I was grieving, still, for Margaret, and now for David too. I was grieving the simplicity I had wanted, and the certainty I had been hoping someone would hand me.

And I was starting to understand what the people I interviewed already knew.

When you are grieving, and when you are dying, and when you are afraid, you do not need correct theology.

You need something to hold.

You need a story that makes the loss survivable.

You need permission to hope even when hope feels irrational.

Maybe that is all heaven ever was.

Not a place.

Not even a belief.

Just permission.

Permission to say death is not the final word.

Permission to say the people I love are not simply gone.

Permission to say reality might be bigger than what I can measure and prove.

People needed that permission.

And the part that frightened me most was realizing I might need it too.

PART IV:

THE PATTERNS – GENERATIONAL

Chapter 11

How Boomers Hold On

I met Robert at a mainline Presbyterian church in Evanston. He was seventy-two, and he had been attending that church for forty-three years.

I asked him whether he believed in heaven.

"Not literally."

"What does that mean?"

He leaned back, as if he had answered this question before, or as if he had been answering it silently for years.

"I think heaven is a metaphor," he said. "A symbol for hope. For the idea that love continues in some form. For the belief that justice will eventually prevail. But do I think there is an actual place where I will go when I die and see my relatives again? No."

"But you still go to church every Sunday."

"Yes."

"Why?"

"Because the metaphor is useful," he said. "It gives me a framework for meaning and mortality. It connects me to a community. It provides rituals that mark important moments in life. I do not need it to be literally true for it to function."

"Does the church know you think this way?"

"Probably not," he said. "But I suspect I am not the only one. Many people my age have revised their beliefs, and they stay because the community matters more than doctrine."

This became one of the clearest patterns I encountered.

Many Boomers remained in religious spaces not because they believed everything taught there, but because they needed connection, ritual, and a sense of belonging to something larger than themselves. Over time, they learned how to hold beliefs loosely enough that disagreement did not require departure.

I met a Catholic woman named Margaret at a parish in Skokie. She was seventy. She had raised four children in the Church and taught religious education for fifteen years.

I asked her if she believed in hell.

"No," she said. "I stopped believing in hell a long time ago. Probably in my forties. The idea that a loving God would create people knowing most would end up in eternal torture never made sense to me."

"But the Church teaches hell."

"The Church teaches many things," she said. "I take what

helps and leave the rest. That's what most Catholics I know do. We're cafeteria Catholics."

"Does that bother the priests?"

"If it does, they don't say anything," she said. "I think they know they would lose half the congregation if they demanded strict belief in every doctrine."

I spoke with Susan at a Lutheran church in Arlington Heights. She was sixty-eight.

"I believe in heaven," she told me, "just not the way I used to."

"What changed?"

"I once thought heaven was literal," she said. "Clouds. Harps. Meeting Jesus. Now I think it's symbolic. A way of speaking about continuation without needing to explain the mechanics."

"So you don't believe you'll actually see your parents again?"

"I don't know," she said. "Maybe I will. Maybe I won't. But I've stopped needing to know. The uncertainty doesn't frighten me the way it once did."

"When did that shift happen?"

"In my fifties," she said. "I realized I had spent decades

trying to be certain about things no one can be certain about, and it was exhausting. So I gave myself permission not to know. To hold it lightly. To remain connected to the tradition without demanding that it be literally true."

The pattern appeared everywhere.

Boomers had been raised with certainty. Many had been taught that doubt was sinful and that questions were dangerous. Yet over time, often quietly and without drama, they revised their beliefs. They no longer believed what they had once been taught, but they stayed anyway.

They showed up on Sundays. They participated in rituals. They said the words. They inhabited the role.

They stayed because community mattered more than theology. They stayed because leaving felt like losing identity. And after forty or fifty years in the same congregation, leaving would have meant not only losing belief but also losing their entire social world.

I met a man named Tom at an evangelical church in Wheaton. He was sixty-nine.

"I don't believe most of what is preached here," he told me. "I don't believe in the rapture. I don't believe in young-earth creationism. I don't believe God sends people to hell for believing the wrong things."

"So why stay?"

"Because these are my people," he said. "I've known them for thirty years. We raised our children together. We've been through marriages, divorces, and deaths together. I'm not leaving over theology."

"Do they know you disagree?"

"Some suspect it," he said. "But we don't talk about it. We talk about grandchildren and golf and the neighborhood. Theology fades into the background. Relationship is what remains."

What I was learning was that many Boomers had developed a sophisticated form of compartmentalization.

Public belief and private belief lived in separate spaces. They could affirm creeds they no longer held because affirmation had become ritual rather than confession. They could participate in practices they still found meaningful even when they no longer accepted the theology behind them.

And they had made peace with that contradiction in a way younger generations often could not, or would not.

But not all Boomers had loosened their grip.

I met Paul at an evangelical church in Wheaton. He was seventy-four. He told me he had been saved at sixteen and had never doubted since.

"Heaven is real," he said. "Not metaphor. Not symbol. It's an actual place where believers go to be with Jesus forever. I know this because the Bible says it, and the Bible is the Word of God."

"You've never doubted?"

"Never," he said. "Doubt comes from Satan. Faith is trusting God even when you don't understand. I've had questions, but never doubt."

I asked about friends or family members who did not believe.

"I pray for them," he said. "I witness to them. I tell them the truth. If they reject it, that's their choice. I can't save anyone. Only Jesus can. But I can point people to Him."

"Do you believe people who don't accept Jesus go to hell?"

"Yes," he said. "That's what Scripture teaches. I don't like it. But I don't get to change God's rules because they make me uncomfortable."

This group existed within the Boomer generation too. People who had held onto certainty. People who had not revised their beliefs. People who believed at seventy what they believed at seventeen.

For them, heaven remained as literal and fixed as it had

always been.

But they were the minority.

I met Barbara at a Methodist church in Naperville. She was sixty-six, a retired elementary school teacher. Her husband Jim had died from pancreatic cancer four years earlier. They had been married for forty-one years.

"Do you believe you will see him again?" I asked.

"Yes," she said without hesitation. "Not because I need to. Because it's true."

I asked what made her certain.

"When Jim was dying, we talked about everything. The things you avoid in your whole marriage suddenly become urgent. And one night, about a week before he passed, he asked me if I believed heaven was real. I said I did. He asked me how I knew."

She paused.

"I told him I didn't know the way you know two plus two equals four. But I knew the way you know someone loves you. You feel it. You experience it. You trust it even without proof."

"Did that satisfy him?"

"He smiled and said, 'Good. Because I'll be waiting for you there.' And I believed him. I still do."

I asked if she had ever wavered since his death.

"The first year was hell," she said. "Absolute hell. I would wake up and forget he was gone. Reach for him in bed. Set two places at the table. The grief was physical. But through all of it, I never stopped believing he was somewhere. That he was okay. That one day I would see him again."

"How did that belief help?"

"It gave me a reason to keep going," she said. "When you lose someone you love that much, you need to believe the separation isn't permanent. Otherwise, what's the point? Why keep waking up? Why keep living?"

She folded her hands.

"I know some people think I'm deluding myself. That I'm using religion as a crutch to avoid facing reality. But this isn't denial. I know Jim's body is in the ground. I know he's not coming back to this life. What I believe is that death isn't the end of him. That his soul, his essence, whatever you want to call it, continues. And that when my time comes, we'll be together again."

"Do you worry you might be wrong?"

"Sometimes," she said. "Late at night when the house is too quiet. But even if I am wrong, the belief carried me through the hardest years of my life. It gave me hope when I had none. It kept me connected to Jim even in his absence. If that's delusion, it's a merciful one. And I'll take mercy over cold truth any day."

Most Boomers I interviewed had traveled from certainty to uncertainty, from rigid belief to flexible hope, from answers to questions they no longer feared.

I met a Jewish woman named Ruth at a synagogue in Highland Park. She was seventy-three and had lost both parents within five years.

"Do you believe in an afterlife?" I asked.

"I don't know," she said. "Judaism doesn't require me to know. I can live a faithful Jewish life without a position on what happens after death."

"But do you hope for something?"

"Of course," she said. "I hope my parents are somewhere. I hope I'll see them again. But hope isn't belief, and belief isn't knowledge. I can hope without pretending to know."

"Does that help with grief?"

"It helps that I don't have to pretend," she said. "When my mother died, people said the usual things. That she was in a better place. That she was at peace. That she was watching over me. I appreciated the kindness, but none of it felt true."

"What felt true was that she was gone, that I missed her, and that I would carry her forward by living well. That was enough."

Across these conversations, one thing became clear.

Boomers are a transitional generation. They were raised with certainty, and many now live with doubt, and they are trying to pass something on without being sure what that something is.

Some hold tightly to what they were taught because loosening their grip feels like losing everything. Others have released certainty but stayed connected to tradition, finding meaning in ritual even when doctrine no longer convinces them. Most live somewhere in between, improvising a faith that works even if it would not satisfy their parents or their pastors.

They are holding on.

Not always to belief, exactly.

They are holding on to the community. They are holding on to ritual. They are holding on to the hope that there might be something after death even if they cannot define it, and even if they no longer trust the old maps the way they once did.

They are the generation that learned to live with uncertainty while still showing up.

The generation that stopped believing literally but kept participating anyway.

The generation that revised almost everything while

changing almost nothing on the outside.

Watching them navigate this tension taught me something important about belief across a lifetime.

Belief is not static. It evolves. It loosens and tightens. It breaks and reforms. Sometimes it grows more precise, and sometimes it becomes more honest by becoming less certain.

And sometimes holding on means letting go of what you once believed while keeping the practices that still connect you to something larger than yourself.

That is what many Boomers are doing.

They stay by reinterpreting. They believe by admitting they do not know. They keep the community even when the doctrine no longer holds.

It is messy. It is contradictory. It is human.

And it may be the most honest form of faith available.

Chapter 12

Gen X'S Quiet Doubt

Sarah was forty-nine. She worked in marketing, and when we met at a coffee shop in Wicker Park, she wore a band T-shirt under a blazer like it was armor.

She opened by saying, "I'm probably the worst person to ask about this. I don't know what I believe, and I'm extremely uncomfortable talking about it."

"That makes you perfect, actually."

She laughed, but she still looked uneasy. "That's the thing. My parents' generation would never admit they don't know. They just say they believe, and that's that. My kids' generation is totally fine with saying they don't know and talking about it for hours. But us? We know we don't know. We're not comfortable pretending we do, but we're also deeply uncomfortable admitting we don't. So we just avoid the topic entirely."

This became the defining characteristic of nearly every Gen X conversation about heaven: an acute awareness of uncertainty paired with a deep discomfort about expressing it.

Sarah's parents were Catholic. Her mother had a detailed

timeline mapped out: purgatory, then heaven, then reunion with Sarah's father. The plan was clear.

"I think she's probably wrong," Sarah said. "But I would never tell her that. What's the point? She's seventy-four. Her belief comforts her. Why would I take that away? But I also can't lie and say I agree with her. So when she talks about it, I nod and change the subject."

"What do you actually believe?"

"I have no idea," she said. "Some days I think there might be something. Some days I think it's all wishful thinking. Most days, I'm just grateful nobody's asking me to commit to an answer."

Gen X avoidance of the heaven question was not apathy.

It was exhausted agnosticism mixed with social anxiety about taking a firm position.

I interviewed a man named David who was forty-six. He had grown up Methodist but had not been to church in twenty years.

"Do you believe in heaven?"

"I'm not sure. I don't disbelieve it, but I don't really believe it," he said. "I don't spend time on the question."

"Why not?"

"Because thinking about it means taking a position," he said.

"And taking a position means either lying to myself or disappointing someone. If I say I believe, I'm lying because I don't. If I say I don't believe, my mom will be devastated. So I just don't engage with the question."

"What happens when someone dies? Do you avoid funerals?"

"I go to funerals," he said. "I say, 'I'm sorry for your loss.' I hug people. I don't say anything about heaven because I don't know how to say something that is both honest and helpful. So I focus on being present."

This pattern appeared everywhere.

Gen X had watched their Boomer parents perform certainty while privately doubting. They had seen the contradictions, and they had seen the hypocrisy, and they had noticed the distance between stated belief and lived behavior. And they had decided not to perform.

But they also had not discovered what to replace the performance with.

So they opted out.

They avoided religious spaces. They changed the subject when the family asked about belief. They attended funerals and said nothing about the afterlife. They lived between their parents' performed certainty and their children's casual uncertainty, and they felt uneasy in both directions.

I met a woman named Jennifer at a brewery in Logan Square. She was forty-four.

"My parents think I'm Christian," she told me. "My kids think I'm agnostic. Both are sort of right and sort of wrong."

"What are you actually?"

"I honestly don't know," she said. "I was raised evangelical. I believed everything until I was about twenty-five. Then doubts crept in. By thirty, I stopped going to church. By thirty-five, I stopped praying. But I've never actually said out loud that I don't believe in God or heaven, because saying it makes it real. And I'm not ready for it to be real."

"Why not?"

"Because my whole identity was built on being Christian," she said. "If I'm not that anymore, then who am I? What do I tell my parents? And what happens when I die? I don't have answers to any of that. So I don't decide. I live in the uncertainty and hope I don't have to resolve it."

What I was discovering was that Gen X had replaced certainty with ambiguity, and then replaced ambiguity with avoidance.

They did not have the decisiveness of atheists who rejected heaven outright.

They did not have the peace of believers who found genuine faith.

They were stuck in the middle, aware that the old frameworks no longer worked, but unable to commit to new ones.

I interviewed a man named Michael who was fifty-one. His father had died two years earlier.

"Did you talk with your dad about what he believed before he died?"

"No."

"Why not?"

"Because we had never talked about it before, and starting that conversation when he was dying felt too heavy," he said. "And honestly, I didn't want to know. If he told me he believed in heaven, I would feel obligated to pretend I agreed. If he told me he was afraid there was nothing, I would feel obligated to comfort him with beliefs I don't have. So we avoided it."

"Do you regret that?"

"Every day," he said. "But I still don't know what I would have said."

Gen X discomfort with heaven was not primarily intellectual.

It was social.

They had been raised in a culture that demanded certainty, and at the same time they developed critical thinking skills that made certainty feel impossible. They were taught that doubt was weakness, and then they lived long enough to realize doubt was unavoidable. So they split the difference by refusing engagement altogether.

I met a woman named Lisa at a coffee shop in Oak Park. She was forty-seven. Her mother had recently been diagnosed with terminal cancer.

"Has she talked to you about what she believes happens after death?"

"She's tried," Lisa said. "She keeps saying she'll see my dad again in heaven. And I just say, 'That's nice,' and change the subject."

"Why not engage?"

"Because if I engage honestly, I'll tell her I don't think heaven exists, and she'll die thinking I'm going to hell," Lisa said. "And if I engage dishonestly, I'll tell her I believe and I'll feel like I lied to my dying mother. So I redirect. We talk about treatment.

We talk about estate planning. We don't talk about what comes after."

"Does she know you're avoiding it?"

"Probably," she said. "But she doesn't push. I think we've both agreed to let it stay unsaid."

What Gen X shared was this.

They could not perform their parents' certainty.

They could not embrace their children's ease with uncertainty.

So they lived in silence.

Aware of doubt. Unable to resolve it. Unwilling to discuss it.

They attended funerals and said the expected words without meaning them. They allowed family members to assume beliefs without correcting them. They stayed away from religious spaces but still carried a vague guilt for doing so, as if leaving the building meant leaving the question. They were the generation caught between frameworks, belonging fully to neither.

And they made peace with that tension by refusing to choose.

I asked Sarah whether she thought she would ever figure out

what she believed.

"Probably not," she said. "And honestly, I'm okay with that. My parents needed answers. My kids don't need answers. I'm in the middle, and the middle is where I'm staying. It's uncomfortable, but it's honest. And that's the best I can do."

Gen X's quiet doubt was not a failure of faith.

It was a refusal to pretend.

They would not perform certainty they did not feel. They would not commit to positions they could not defend. They would not force resolution on questions that might not have answers.

They lived without knowing.

And they did it quietly.

Without declarations. Without confrontation. Without needing validation or correction.

Gen X learned to be comfortable being uncomfortable.

And in a culture that demanded certainty from every direction, that, too, was a form of courage.

Chapter 13
Millennials Redesign Everything

I met Tyler at a coffee shop in Pilsen that sold both oat milk and crystals at the counter, which felt like perfect Millennial territory. He was thirty-four, worked in tech, had a lotus flower tattoo on his forearm, and he opened with a question that sounded rehearsed.

"So I'm spiritual but not religious. Does that count for your project?"

"It counts."

"Cool," he said, relieved. "Because I have thoughts about heaven, but they're not, like, traditional thoughts."

That became the opening line for almost every Millennial conversation. They all had thoughts about heaven. None of them were traditional. And almost all of them wanted to say, upfront, that their beliefs were personalized, evolving, and probably would not make sense to their parents.

Tyler's version of heaven went like this. Consciousness does not end at death. It transforms. The individual self dissolves, but the energy that made up your awareness returns to a universal field. You are not you anymore, but you are not gone either. You become part of everything. And that, he said, is better than being a separate self, because separation is what causes suffering.

"Did you get this from Buddhism?"

"Sort of," he said. "I've read some Buddhism. I've done meditation retreats. I follow some teachers on Instagram. But I've also taken pieces from other traditions. Like, I think reincarnation is probably real, but not the way Hindus describe it. More like your energy gets recycled into new forms, and maybe some patterns carry over, but it's not like you come back as a specific person with memories."

"So you've constructed your own cosmology."

"I mean, yeah," he said. "Isn't that what everyone does? You take the parts that resonate, you discard the parts that don't, and you build something that works for you."

"But how do you know any of it is true?"

He looked at me like I had asked a strange question. "I don't know if it's true. I just know it feels right. It makes me less afraid of death. That's enough."

That phrase came up constantly with Millennials: it feels right.

Not "it's true." Not "Scripture says." Not "the church

teaches." Just "it feels right."

Millennials had grown up in an era of religious pluralism. They were exposed to multiple traditions and multiple truth claims that contradicted each other. Many of them reached the same conclusion: if everyone claims to have the truth and the claims conflict, then either nobody has the full truth, or everybody has a piece of it, or truth itself is more flexible than earlier generations assumed.

So they gave themselves permission to construct belief systems out of whatever resonated personally.

Jessica, thirty-one, described her version of heaven like this: "It's like a higher dimension where consciousness exists without physical form. You're reunited with people you love, but not in bodies. More like your essences merge, or something. And there's no judgment because judgment is a human thing. God, or the universe, or whatever you want to call it, doesn't judge. It just loves. And that love is what heaven is. Just being held in unconditional love forever."

"Where does this come from?"

"I've read some near-death experience accounts," she said. "I've listened to podcasts about consciousness. I've done psychedelics that gave me experiences of ego dissolution, and it felt like what I imagine death might be like. I combined all of that into something that makes sense to me."

"Does this contradict your Christian upbringing?"

"Oh, completely," she said. "My parents think I lost my faith. But I don't think I lost it. I think I evolved it. The God they worship is judgmental and demanding, and you have to believe exactly the right things or you go to hell. That God doesn't make sense to me. But a God who is pure love and acceptance does. So I kept the love part and discarded the judgment part."

What struck me was how consistent the patterns were, even though everyone insisted their beliefs were unique.

Almost everyone eliminated hell, or at least eternal torment. Some kept a temporary purification process. Some kept the idea that you had to work through your issues before reaching full peace. But almost none of them believed anyone was tortured forever.

"Because that's messed up," as one twenty-eight-year-old named Marcus put it. "If God is love, and love never gives up, then hell doesn't make sense. You can't claim God loves everyone and then say God tortures some people forever. That isn't love. That's abuse. So either the traditional teaching is wrong, or the God being described isn't actually loving."

Almost everyone eliminated specific religious requirements. You did not have to accept Jesus, follow Muhammad, be baptized, or say the right prayers. Good people went to heaven regardless of affiliation. The mechanism was usually something vague about intention, or love, or energy, or consciousness.

Almost everyone made heaven more customizable. Not one heaven everyone shares, but personalized experiences shaped by what each individual needs. Your heaven might be different from my heaven, and that was fine. The universe is infinite, so there is room for everyone's version.

And almost everyone emphasized the same phrase: no judgment.

It came up so often I started counting. In fifty-seven Millennial interviews, forty-three people said some version of "heaven has no judgment," or "God doesn't judge," or "judgment is a human construct that doesn't exist in the afterlife."

I asked Maya, twenty-nine, why it mattered so much.

"Because judgment is toxic," she said. "Growing up, everything was about judgment. Am I good enough? Am I saved? Am I doing the right things? Did I believe the right way? It was constant anxiety about whether I measured up. That's not healthy. That's not what spirituality should be. Spirituality should be about acceptance and love and growth, not constantly worrying whether you're good enough for God."

"But doesn't some kind of moral accounting make sense?" I asked. "Shouldn't Hitler and Mr. Rogers have different experiences in the afterlife?"

She thought for a moment. "Maybe. But I don't think it's about punishment. I think it's more like people who hurt others carry that weight into the afterlife, and they have to process it and heal from it. And eventually everyone heals and everyone is okay. Because infinite punishment for finite crimes is unjust. And if the universe is unjust, then there's no point to any of this."

The Millennial reconstruction of heaven was fundamentally therapeutic.

Previous generations tended to frame heaven as reward, restoration, or reunion. Millennials framed it as healing. It was where trauma got processed, where wounds got mended, where you finally became whole.

Chris, thirty-two, told me, "I think heaven is where you work through all your stuff. Like therapy, but infinite, and it actually works. You confront what you did wrong. You understand why you did it. You forgive yourself and others. And eventually you reach total acceptance and peace. But it's not instant. It's a process."

"How long does the process take?"

"I don't know," he said. "Maybe years. Maybe centuries.

Maybe time works differently there. However long it takes, that's how long it takes. The point isn't to rush. The point is to heal."

This therapeutic framing showed up everywhere. Heaven was not about singing hymns forever or worshiping at the throne of God. It was about becoming integrated. Releasing shame. Letting go of fear. Finally being okay with yourself.

One woman described it as "the place where you finally get to rest from performing. You don't have to pretend anymore. You don't have to maintain an image. You just get to be yourself, completely, and be loved exactly as you are."

When I asked whether therapy culture influenced this, she laughed.

"Oh absolutely. I've been in therapy for eight years. I've done EMDR for trauma. I've worked on attachment issues. Of course that shapes how I think about the afterlife. If this life is about healing and growing, then maybe the afterlife is continuing that process, just without the limits of the body and the pressure of society."

What fascinated me was how confidently Millennials stated these beliefs while also admitting they could not prove them. I would ask, "How do you know this is what happens?"

And they would say, "I don't know for sure, but it makes

sense. And I've had experiences that confirm it for me."

The experiences varied. Psychedelic trips. Meditation insights. Dreams that felt significant. Synchronicities that seemed meaningful. A sense of presence from a dead loved one. An intuitive certainty they described as "just knowing."

None of it would satisfy a philosopher or theologian as evidence. But Millennials were rarely trying to build a rigorous argument. They were trying to build something livable.

I met Daniel, thirty-three, who told me reincarnation was real because he had done a past-life regression and remembered being a soldier in World War I.

"Do you think that was a real memory," I asked, "or your imagination?"

He shrugged. "Does it matter? It felt real. It helped me understand patterns in my life. Whether it was literally true or metaphorically true, it was useful."

That pragmatic approach came up constantly. Truth claims were evaluated less by correspondence to reality and more by what they produced in a person's life.

If believing in reincarnation makes you less afraid of death and more intentional about your choices, then believe in reincarnation.

If believing in universal consciousness makes you feel connected and less alone, then believe in universal consciousness.

If believing in ancestor spirits helps you maintain a relationship with your dead, then believe in ancestor spirits.

The question was not "Is it true?" The question was "Does it help?"

What Millennials had done was democratize theology.

They took authority away from institutions and handed it to individuals. You did not need a priest, a pastor, or a sacred text to tell you what heaven is. You could figure it out yourself based on your own experiences and intuition.

This drove older generations crazy.

I showed a Boomer my notes from a Millennial interview, and he said, "This is nonsense. You can't just make up your own theology. There's tradition. There's Scripture. Two thousand years of people who have thought about this more deeply than some thirty-year-old with an Instagram account."

Millennials would answer, "Those traditions contradict each other. Scripture gets interpreted a thousand ways. And the people two thousand years ago didn't know anything we don't. They were guessing too. I'm doing the same thing with different inputs."

The shift in authority was complete. Truth was not what the

institution said. Truth was what felt right to you, validated by your experience, confirmed by your intuition.

I met with a group of Millennials at a meditation center in Andersonville. Eight people, ages twenty-seven to thirty-eight, all involved in spiritual practices and none affiliated with traditional religion.

I asked them, "What do you think happens when you die?"

The answers came fast.

"Your consciousness merges with the universal field."

"You review your life and integrate the lessons."

"You reunite with your soul family."

"You choose whether to reincarnate or move to a higher dimension."

"You dissolve into pure awareness."

"You return to source energy."

"You enter a space of infinite healing and love."

"You become one with everything."

I asked, "Do any of you believe in the traditional Christian heaven? Streets of gold, seeing Jesus, worshiping God forever?"

They all shook their heads.

One woman, Rachel, said, "That vision of heaven was created by people in a specific time and place with specific concerns. Streets of gold made sense to people who were poor. Eternal rest made sense to people who were physically exhausted. Reunion made sense to people who had lost loved ones to disease and war. But we live in a different time. We have different needs, so we need a different vision."

"But how do you know your vision is more accurate than theirs?"

"We don't," she said. "We're all guessing. But at least we're honest about it. We're saying this is what makes sense to me, instead of claiming God revealed it and you have to believe it or you're damned. That feels humbler."

The Millennial relationship with doubt was also different. They were not afraid of doubt. They treated it as evidence of growth.

Alex, thirty-five, told me, "I've changed what I believe about the afterlife five times in ten years. I'll probably change it again. Beliefs should evolve as you learn. Being certain at twenty-five about what happens after death seems arrogant. How would I know? I haven't died yet."

"But doesn't uncertainty make it hard to live?" I asked. "Don't you need a stable foundation?"

"The foundation is that consciousness continues in some form," he said. "The details are negotiable. Some days reincarnation makes sense. Some days it feels more like merging with something larger. Some days I wonder if it's all brain chemistry and there's nothing after. I don't need to pick one and commit forever. I can hold the possibilities and see what fits as I get older."

That kind of fluidity would have been unthinkable in earlier generations. They wanted an answer. Millennials were comfortable with maybe.

One conversation captured their approach perfectly.

Lauren, thirty, described a complex system involving soul contracts, reincarnation, dimensional beings, energy healing, and eventual merger with source consciousness. When I asked where she learned it, she said she had read near-death accounts, listened to teachers, tried plant medicine, had experiences in meditation, and then synthesized it into a model that made sense to her.

I asked, "Do you think this is objectively true? Like if we could measure the afterlife scientifically, would it match your description?"

She paused. "Probably not exactly. I'm sure some of what I believe is wrong or incomplete. But it's the best model I have right now with the information I've got. And it's way better than the model I was given growing up, which was believe in Jesus or burn forever. That model is morally repugnant and psychologically damaging. So even if my current model is wrong, at least it isn't harmful."

"So your criterion is not harmful, rather than true."

"My criterion is," she said, "does this belief make me more loving, more compassionate, more at peace? Does it help me live better and fear death less? Does it connect me to others or isolate me? If it helps, then it's useful. I'll worry about absolute truth when I die and find out what's actually happening."

After months of Millennial interviews, I understood what they had done.

They had taken heaven apart and rebuilt it from scratch using whatever materials were available: Buddhism, Christianity, New Age spirituality, near-death experience stories, therapy language, psychedelic insights, and intuition. Sometimes they added misunderstood pop-science concepts because they sounded like proof. Sometimes they admitted they were guessing and did it anyway.

The result was messy and contradictory, and it was entirely personal.

But it was theirs.

And it worked for them.

They were not waiting for an institution to tell them what to believe. They were not bound by tradition or Scripture or authority. They were building meaning from the ground up.

Was it true? They did not know.

Did it help? Yes.

And for Millennials, that was enough.

But not every Millennial went the DIY route.

I met Elena at a Catholic church in Logan Square. She was thirty-one, a high school history teacher. She had grown up in a secular household. Her parents were academics who considered religion superstition. She did not attend church as a child. She was not baptized. By her own description, she was raised to believe religion was for people who could not handle reality.

Then she joined the Catholic Church at twenty-six.

"What happened?" I asked.

"I spent my twenties constructing my own spirituality," she said. "Exactly like everyone else in my generation. I took pieces from Buddhism, Stoicism, and some vague pantheism. I meditated. I journaled. I read books about consciousness. And I felt empty the entire time."

"Why?"

"Because nothing I constructed felt solid. It was all just me, projecting my preferences onto the universe and calling it truth. I could make it mean whatever I wanted it to mean, and that flexibility started to feel hollow. If I were making it all up, then none of it mattered."

She paused.

"Then a friend invited me to Mass. I went out of curiosity, maybe to mock it a little. But something happened. The liturgy, the ritual, the sense that I was participating in something two thousand years old that had nothing to do with me or my feelings or my preferences. It was bigger than me. It existed before I was born and would exist after I died. And that felt like relief."

"Relief from what?"

"From the exhausting work of being my own authority," she said. "From having to decide what was true based on nothing but my own intuition. I wanted something that made claims. Something that said this is how it is, not this is how you want it to be."

I asked about heaven. About what she believed now.

"I believe what the Church teaches. Heaven is union with God. Full communion with the Trinity. The beatific vision. Not floating on clouds. Not playing harps. Just being in the presence of infinite love and truth and beauty forever. And I believe hell is real.

Not fire and torture, but separation from God by choice. If you reject love your whole life, then the afterlife is the logical conclusion of that rejection."

"That's a harder teaching than most Millennials accept. Does it trouble you?"

"It did at first," she said. "But the more I understood it, the more it made sense. Hell isn't God punishing people. It's people choosing separation. C. S. Lewis said the gates of hell are locked from the inside. That resonates. God offers love to everyone. Some people reject it. They get what they choose."

"But eternal separation? Forever?"

"I don't know how eternity works," she said. "I don't know whether someone in hell could eventually choose differently. The Church leaves room for mystery there. What I do know is that God is both perfectly loving and perfectly just, and somehow those two attributes work together in ways I can't fully comprehend. And I'm okay not comprehending. That's the point of faith."

I asked how her parents reacted.

"They think I had a psychological breakdown," she said, laughing. "My dad keeps sending me articles about religious indoctrination. My mom thinks I'm regressing because I can't handle uncertainty. They don't understand that I tried to be uncertain. I lived in it for years. And I found something sturdier."

"What did you find?"

"Truth that exists independently of me," she said. "A tradition tested by millions of people over centuries. A structure that holds when my feelings don't. I'm not making it up as I go anymore. I'm submitting to something greater than myself. And that submission, paradoxically, is what freed me."

She leaned forward.

"Here's what I learned. My generation is terrified of authority. We don't trust institutions. We don't trust people who claim to know things we don't. So we rejected all external authority and made ourselves the authority. But that's exhausting and destabilizing. At some point, you have to trust something outside yourself, or you're just making it up forever. And I got tired of making it up."

I asked if she ever doubted.

"All the time," she said. "But doubt and faith coexist. Doubt asks the questions. Faith gives the framework to ask them within. I don't need absolute certainty. I need something worth trusting. And the Church, for all its failures, has that. It's stood for two thousand years. It survived empires, plagues, corruption, and stupidity. It must be connected to something real. So I trust it, even when I don't fully understand, and that trust has given me more peace than a decade of DIY spirituality ever did."

After months of Millennial interviews, I understood the larger pattern.

They democratized the afterlife. They made peace with uncertainty. They eliminated judgment and prioritized healing over worship. They redesigned heaven to be therapeutic rather than punitive, fluid rather than fixed, and personalized rather than universal.

Whether they were wiser than their parents or simply building comforting stories tailored to their own psychological needs, I still did not know.

But they had created something new, something that would have been unrecognizable to previous generations, and something that was unmistakably Millennial.

Heaven redesigned for wellness culture.

The afterlife is redesigned as personal growth.

God redesigned as nonjudgmental love.

It was brilliant or delusional or both.

And watching them build it with such earnest confidence was one of the most fascinating things I witnessed in the entire project.

Chapter 14

Gen Z Doesn't Pretend

I met Zara at a bubble tea place in Hyde Park, near the University of Chicago campus where she was a junior studying neuroscience. She was twenty, had dyed green hair, and when I asked what she believed about heaven, she said, "Honestly? Probably nothing. But I'm open to being wrong."

That became the Gen Z template: radical honesty about not knowing, and almost no anxiety about admitting it.

"Tell me more."

"Okay," she said. "So scientifically, consciousness is generated by the brain, right? And when the brain stops, consciousness stops. That's what the evidence suggests. So when you die, you probably just stop existing. It's like before you were born. You weren't anywhere then, and you won't be anywhere after. It's just nothing."

"Does that scare you?"

She stirred her drink and thought about it. "Not really. I can't be scared of something I won't experience. If I'm dead, I won't be around to be upset about being dead. The scary part is thinking about the people I love dying. Like my grandma. She's eighty-four. When she dies, she's probably just gone, and that sucks. But pretending she's going to heaven doesn't actually help me, because I don't believe it. So I'd rather just be sad about the real loss than comfort myself with something I think is fake."

"Your grandma probably believes in heaven."

"Oh, she definitely does," Zara said. "She's Catholic. She goes to Mass every week. And that's fine for her. If it makes her less afraid of death, great. I'm not going to tell her she's wrong. But I'm also not going to pretend I believe it just to make her feel better. That feels condescending."

This refusal to perform belief was the defining characteristic of almost every Gen Z conversation I had. Older generations developed elaborate strategies for navigating religious difference. Boomers often performed certainty even when they carried doubt. Gen X stayed quiet because they did not want conflict. Millennials built personalized hybrids that borrowed from multiple traditions.

Gen Z just said, "I don't believe that," and moved on.

No apology. No extended explanations. No need to soften it with careful language. They would admit uncertainty, but they did not wrap it in guilt.

I met Ethan, twenty-two, who told me he had been an atheist

since he was fourteen.

"How did your parents react?"

"They were worried at first," he said. "They thought it was a phase. They brought me to their pastor, and the pastor tried to convince me that God was real and that I'd go to hell if I didn't believe."

"And what did you do?"

"I said, okay, but none of your arguments are convincing. And threatening me with hell doesn't make your claims more credible. It just makes you sound manipulative."

"You said that to a pastor?"

"Yeah," Ethan said, almost amused. "He didn't know what to do with it. He was used to people who were afraid of hell, or at least people who pretended to be. But I wasn't afraid. If I don't think hell is real, then threatening me with it is like threatening me with the Boogeyman."

"And your parents?"

"They eventually accepted it," he said. "They still go to church. I don't. We don't talk about it much. They know where I stand, and I know where they stand, and we've agreed to disagree."

What struck me was how ordinary this sounded to him. There was no dramatic rupture. No identity crisis. No sense that he was committing a betrayal.

I kept noticing this difference.

When Boomers left the church, it often felt like a rupture with family expectations and a rejection of an entire upbringing. When Gen X drifted away, it often came with guilt, as if they were failing at something they were supposed to be able to do. When Millennials deconstructed, it often became a full emotional project. They talked about religious trauma and unlearning and rebuilding.

But when Gen Z said, "I don't believe in God," it usually landed like a simple statement of fact.

More like, "I don't like cilantro."

I met Emma, nineteen, who grew up in an evangelical church and stopped believing around sixteen.

"What happened at sixteen?"

"Nothing specific," she said. "I just started actually thinking about what they were teaching instead of accepting it. And once I started thinking about it, it fell apart quickly. They say God is all-loving and all-powerful, but there's massive suffering in the world. Those claims don't fit together. Either God isn't all-powerful and can't stop suffering, or God isn't all-loving and won't stop suffering, or God doesn't exist. And the third option seemed most likely."

"Did you talk to your youth pastor about it?"

"Yeah," she said. "He gave me the standard answers. Free will. The Fall. God's plan. Suffering builds character. And I was like, these aren't answers. They're rationalizations. You're trying to make the evidence fit the conclusion."

"What did he say?"

"He said I needed faith," Emma said. "He said not everything can be understood with logic, and God's ways are higher than our ways. And I thought, okay, so when logic contradicts your belief, I'm supposed to abandon logic. That's the opposite of how knowledge works."

"So you left."

"Yeah," she said. "And it was a relief. I'd been pretending for a while because I didn't want to upset my parents. But once I said it out loud, I felt lighter. Like I didn't have to keep performing something I didn't feel."

The Gen Z approach to death and the afterlife tended to be starkly materialist. They talked about consciousness like it was software running on hardware. If the hardware fails, the software ends. There is no ghost in the machine. There is just the machine.

I met a group of college students at Northwestern, six of them, nineteen to twenty-two, and they spoke about death with a casualness that made me uneasy. Not because they were cruel, but because they were unromantic.

I asked what they thought happened after death.

"Nothing," one of them said. "Your neurons stop firing, and your consciousness ends. That's it."

"Probably nothing," another said. "Like ninety percent sure it's nothing. But I guess there could be something we don't understand yet about consciousness. I'm just not counting on it."

"I hope there's nothing," Amir said, and that stopped me.

"You hope there's nothing?"

"Yeah," he said. "Because if there's something, then it goes on forever. And forever is terrifying. Eternal life sounds exhausting. Eventually you'd experience everything, learn everything, do everything, and then what? You just exist forever with nothing new. That's horror."

The others nodded. Nobody looked shocked. For them, infinity was not a consolation prize. It was a threat.

"But what about seeing loved ones again?" I asked.

"I mean, that would be nice," Mia said. "But wanting something doesn't make it true. I want there to be cures for every disease and unlimited clean energy and world peace. Reality doesn't care what I want. If consciousness ends at death, then it ends."

Gen Z was not hostile to the idea of an afterlife. They just wanted evidence. In the absence of evidence, they defaulted to the explanation that required the fewest assumptions.

Jay, twenty-one, put it bluntly. "Show me one verifiable instance of consciousness existing without a physical brain, and I'll reconsider. Show me one near-death experience that includes information the person couldn't have known, and then have it verified by independent observers, and show that it can't be explained by neurological processes. Give me data. Until then, I'm going with the simplest explanation. Consciousness is brain activity, and when brain activity ends, consciousness ends."

"But absence of evidence isn't evidence of absence."

"Sure," he said. "But when you're making an extraordinary claim, the burden of proof is on you. Near-death experiences can be explained by brain chemistry. Medium have been tested and they don't hold up under controlled conditions. Reincarnation stories fall apart when you investigate them. So yeah, maybe there's something we can't detect yet. But I'm not going to believe it until there's actual evidence."

This evidential framework showed up repeatedly. They knew cognitive biases. They could name motivated reasoning. They had grown up fact-checking everything. They brought that same posture to religious claims and found them thin.

What surprised me was that they did not seem angry about it.

They were not trying to fight believers. They were not recruiting people into atheism. They were not staging rebellions against religion.

They were mostly just uninterested.

Religion, for many of them, felt like a legacy technology. Not evil. Not necessarily ridiculous. Just not necessary.

I met Priya, twenty, who told me her parents were Hindu. They did pujas at home and believed in karma and reincarnation.

“And you?”

“I respect it,” she said. “It’s their culture. It’s meaningful to them. But it’s not mine. I respect it like I respect their taste in music. It doesn’t have to matter to me.”

“Do they want you to be Hindu?”

“Kind of,” she said. “But they also raised me to think critically. So when I say I don’t believe in reincarnation because there isn’t any evidence, they can’t really argue. They taught me to value logic and evidence. Now I’m applying those tools to their beliefs.”

“Does it create conflict?”

"Not really," she said. "We just don't talk about it much. They know I'm not religious. I know they are. It's not a big deal."

That détente showed up again and again. Gen Z opted out of belief, and their parents, often Gen X, were too tired to wage a war over it. Both sides seemed to accept the reality and move forward.

The place Gen Z did get animated was hell.

Not because it offended their logic, although it did, but because it offended their moral instincts. They found eternal torment not just false, but ugly.

I was talking with a group of students near DePaul when I mentioned that some Christians and many Muslims believed in eternal punishment for non-believers.

Keisha, a student with a nose ring and an expression that sharpened instantly, said, "That's evil. If I created beings, gave them limited information, made belief in me non-obvious, and then tortured them forever for not believing, I'd be a monster. Any God who does that isn't worth worshiping even if he exists."

"But what if that is just what God is?" I asked. "What if the universe is run by a being who judges that way?"

"Then the universe is run by a tyrant," she said, "and resisting that tyrant is the moral thing to do, even if it means going to hell."

The others agreed. For many of them, the argument was not about whether hell was real. It was about whether worship would be moral even if it were.

Despite the skepticism, Gen Z was not entirely closed to mystery. They were often open to the idea that consciousness could be stranger than current science can explain. They just refused to turn that openness into confident belief.

Jasmine, twenty-two, said, “I don’t think there’s a Christian heaven or a Hindu cycle of rebirth or any of the traditional stuff. But consciousness is weird. Reality is weird. We don’t really understand what consciousness is or where it comes from. So maybe there’s something we’re missing. I’m not ruling it out. I’m just not believing it without evidence.”

“Do you hope there’s something?” I asked.

“I don’t know if I hope for it exactly,” she said. “If there’s nothing, I won’t be around to be disappointed. But if there is something, I hope it isn’t like any religion describes it. I hope it’s weirder. I hope it’s something we can’t imagine with our current framework.”

That was another recurring Gen Z posture: mild openness without commitment. “Interesting if true,” but not “true.”

The most honest conversation I had with Gen Z was with

Devon, twenty-one, whose grandmother had terminal cancer.

"What do you think happens to her when she dies?"

"I think she stops existing," he said. "Her brain stops working, her consciousness ends, and she's gone. That's what I think actually happens."

"And what do you say when she talks about seeing your grandfather again in heaven?"

"I say I hope she's right," he said, without hesitation. "Because what else am I going to do, correct her while she's dying? I'm not that kind of person."

"So you lie."

"No," he said. "I hope she's right. That's not a lie. Hope and belief aren't the same thing. I can hope for something I don't believe is likely."

"Does that feel dishonest?"

He looked at me, and his face softened. "The honest thing would be telling her I think death is final. But honesty isn't always kind. And I'd rather be kind than honest when someone I love is dying. If believing in heaven makes it easier for her, then I'm not going to take that away."

When I left that conversation, I kept thinking about how close it was to something I had heard from older people, even though the vocabulary was different. Different generations, same moral problem. What do you owe the dying? Truth, or comfort? And can you offer comfort without betraying yourself?

After months of talking to Gen Z, I understood what made them different from everyone else.

They were raised in an era of information abundance. They could access every religion, every critique, every documentary about how doctrine evolved, every argument about why belief persists. They had seen the machinery. And many of them concluded, quietly and without drama, that the machinery probably does not point to literal truth.

But they were not grieving heaven.

They were not scrambling for replacements.

They were not trying to turn uncertainty into something prettier.

They were simply willing to say: I don't know, and I'm okay with that.

They did not need heaven to function. They could grieve without it. They could face mortality without dressing it up.

They were sad when people died, and they missed them, and they told stories, and they carried them forward. But they did not require a cosmology to make that grief legitimate.

They accepted loss as loss.

It was brutal and honest, and it was also strangely calm.

Gen Z looked at the universe and seemed to say: You do not owe us an afterlife.

And then they kept living anyway.

No performance. No ritual certainty. No elaborate metaphysics.

Just: this is what I think, based on what I can know, and I won't pretend otherwise.

Heaven?

Probably not real.

And for them, that was not a crisis.

It was just a fact they could live with.

PART V:
WHAT IF THEY'RE RIGHT?

Chapter 15

The Case For Heaven

Months into my research, I realized I had a problem.

I had spent eighteen months documenting doubt. I had spoken with hundreds of people about their private uncertainties. I had collected stories of performed certainty and quiet confusion. And I had avoided, almost reflexively, the strongest intellectual arguments for heaven.

I had talked with believers, but mostly ordinary believers. People shaped by family faith, inherited tradition, or lived experience. Those conversations mattered, and they were the heart of what I was writing. Still, I could not ignore what I had not done.

I had not engaged the theologians and philosophers who built careful cases for life after death. I had documented the weakness of popular belief while sidestepping the strength of serious theology.

That was not honest.

If I were going to write about heaven, I would have to understand the best arguments for it. Not the simplified versions that appear on sympathy cards. The difficult ones. The ones that demand more of you than comfort.

So I started reading.

N. T. Wright first. Then C. S. Lewis. Then David Bentley Hart. Then Eastern Orthodox theology. Then back through the early church fathers.

What surprised me was not that these thinkers believed in heaven. It was that their version looked nothing like the version I had been documenting.

It was stranger. More demanding. More internally coherent.

And it was harder to dismiss.

Wright: Heaven as restoration, not escape

N. T. Wright argues that much of Christianity has misunderstood heaven for centuries. The popular version is familiar. You die, you leave earth, and you float somewhere "up there" forever. Wright says that is not the center of the Christian story.

The center is resurrection. New creation. Heaven coming to earth, not souls escaping earth to reach heaven.

He points to the final chapters of Revelation, where the New Jerusalem descends and God dwells with humanity in a renewed world. The dead are raised, not as free-floating spirits, but as embodied beings in a transformed creation. In that reading, heaven is not a distant destination. It is this world healed and restored, with everything broken repaired.

There is still death, and there is still an intermediate state, a waiting. But the final horizon is not escape. It is renewal.

This was not the heaven I kept hearing about in coffee shops and hospital hallways. This was not just a coping mechanism. It was a claim about what reality is doing.

Wright ties it to the resurrection of Jesus. He treats it as the turning point that signals restoration has begun, that death has been interrupted, and that the trajectory of the universe is not ultimately decay, but renewal.

I could not verify any of this. I also could not dismiss it as naive. It was a framework built with care, grounded in texts that millions of people have taken seriously for two thousand years. And if it were true, it would mean the losses I had been documenting were not the final word.

Lewis: Desire as a clue

C. S. Lewis makes a different kind of argument, and it begins with desire.

If I find in myself a desire that nothing in this world can satisfy, Lewis says, then the most probable explanation is that I was made for another world.

He is not saying that wanting something proves it exists. He is not claiming that longing manufactures reality. He is making a more subtle point. Natural desires tend to correspond to real objects.

We experience hunger, and food exists. We experience thirst, and water exists. We experience sexual desire, and sex exists. And we experience a deeper longing that seems to outlast every fulfillment. Even our best moments feel as if they point beyond themselves. We get what we wanted, and then the wanting returns. Not because we are ungrateful, but because the thing we wanted was never quite the thing we were longing for.

Lewis argues that this longing is not proof, but it may be evidence. It might be diagnostic. It might reveal something about what human beings are made for.

I had never taken this seriously. I had assumed longing for heaven was fear of death wearing nicer clothes.

But Lewis suggested something else. What if longing is not only psychological, but also perceptual? What if some desires are not just coping strategies, but signals?

I thought about the people I had interviewed. The children built heavens that solved the problem of harm. The grieving parents who could not release the idea of reunion. The dying patients who described a kind of peace that did not sound like denial.

What if their longing was not only a defense mechanism?

What if it was also an interpretation of something real, something I could not perceive because I had trained myself to mistrust it?

I did not know. But I could no longer dismiss the question as easily as I had.

Hart: Love cannot end in death

David Bentley Hart does not argue like Lewis. He does not begin with yearning. He begins with metaphysics, and he is almost surgical about it.

In his work on the problem of evil and the nature of God, he makes an argument that stayed with me after I closed the book.

If God is love, and if love is the deepest reality of existence, then death cannot be the final word.

Because death is not just a biological shutdown. It is separation. It is the tearing apart of a relationship. It is the annihilation of communion. It is, in a sense, violence against love itself.

Hart's claim is not that heaven exists because people need comfort. His claim is that if Christianity's description of God is true, then some form of restoration must exist. Otherwise, the entire framework collapses. A God who is love cannot create beings for communion and then allow communion to be permanently erased by death.

He does not pretend this can be proven in a lab. He treats it as a matter of coherence. Either love is ultimate, or death is. One of them must give way.

I could not accept the premise without question, and I knew that. I did not have a settled account of God. But what struck me was the shape of the argument. It was not sentimental. It was not an attempt to soothe. It was logic built on a claim about reality.

And it forced me to see how quickly I had dismissed serious belief as mere psychology.

Eastern Orthodox thought: Theosis

Eastern Orthodox theology offered a framework unlike anything I had been expecting. Not heaven as a place you go. Not heaven as payment for good behavior.

Theosis. Union with God. Participation in divine life.

In this vision, the goal is not disembodied survival. The goal is transformation. Becoming fully alive through communion with God, and being transfigured within creation rather than removed from it. Death is not the finish line. It is a passage within a larger process of becoming.

This was the strangest vision I encountered, and it was also, in its own way, the most demanding.

Not a static eternity. Not a reward you collect.

An ongoing deepening. More alive. More conscious. More fully yourself, not less.

Again, I had no way to verify it. But I could not pretend it was shallow. It did not read like wish fulfillment. It read like a tradition that had been thinking for centuries about what it would mean for God to be real and for humans to be made for more than decay.

The false binary I had been living with

The more I read, the more I realized I had been operating with a narrow set of options.

Either consciousness ends at death.

Or souls go to heaven.

But these thinkers were proposing something else entirely.

Resurrection, not the immortality of the soul. Transformation, not mere preservation. New creation, not escape from creation. Participation, not passive reward.

These were not folk beliefs. They were intellectual traditions, built slowly, argued over, refined, and handed down.

They might be wrong. I could not assume they were right. But I could no longer call them simple comfort stories.

But I also met people who lived these arguments.

I met Thomas at a lecture series on philosophy of mind at Northwestern. He was sixty-one, a professor of neuroscience who had spent three decades studying consciousness. He also believed in heaven.

"How does a neuroscientist believe in an afterlife?" I asked.

"Because consciousness is the hardest problem in science," he said. "We can map neural correlates. We can track activity patterns. We can predict responses. But we cannot explain why any of that produces subjective experience. Why there is something it is like to be you."

He leaned forward.

"Materialism assumes consciousness is produced by the brain. But we have no mechanism for how matter generates experience. We assume it does because experience correlates with brain states. That is correlation, not causation. And the explanatory gap has not closed in fifty years of research."

"So you think consciousness is non-physical?"

"I think consciousness might be fundamental," he said. "Not generated by matter, but inherent to reality. And if consciousness is fundamental, then death might not end it. The brain might be a filter or receiver, not a generator. When the brain dies, consciousness continues, just not in the same form."

"That sounds like wishful thinking dressed up as science."

"It sounds that way until you study the actual data," he said. "Near-death experiences. Terminal lucidity in dementia patients who suddenly become clear moments before death. Veridical perceptions during cardiac arrest when the brain shows no activity. None of this proves survival. But it suggests our model of consciousness might be incomplete."

He paused.

"I am not certain heaven exists. I am certain materialism has not explained consciousness. And in that gap, belief becomes reasonable, not delusional."

I met Jennifer at a grief support group in Evanston. She was fifty-three, a lawyer. She had been clinically dead for four minutes after a car accident eight years earlier, and she told me she had seen something.

"What did you see?"

"Light. But not regular light. It was alive somehow. And I felt completely known. Like everything I had ever done, thought, or felt was visible, and I was loved anyway. Not judged. Just loved."

"Do you think that was real, or your brain shutting down?"

"I have asked that question every day for eight years," she said. "I have read the neuroscience. I know about oxygen deprivation. I know the brain can create experiences during trauma. But what I experienced felt more real than this conversation. More real than anything before or since."

She looked directly at me.

"Here is what I know. I was afraid of death before the accident. Terrified. After I came back, the fear was gone. Not because I talked myself into something. Because I experienced something that changed me at a level I cannot undo. Whether it was heaven or my brain's final gift to me, it worked. I live differently now. I am kinder. I care less about accumulation. I take people seriously because I believe I will see them again."

"So even if it was a hallucination, it functioned as truth?"

"Maybe," she said. "Or maybe the materialist explanation is the hallucination, and what I saw was the first real thing I had ever encountered. I do not need you to believe me. I just need to tell you that death is not what I thought it was. And if I am right, then everyone you interviewed who dismissed heaven might be wrong."

I met Father Michael at an Episcopal church in Hyde Park. He was seventy-one, had been a priest for forty-six years, and had sat with hundreds of dying people.

"Do you believe in heaven because the Church teaches it, or because you have seen evidence?"

"Both," he said. "The Church teaching gave me language. Sitting with the dying gave me something else."

"What?"

"Peace that makes no sense," he said. "I have watched people die in agony, and then suddenly go calm. Not from morphine. Something else. And I have heard dying people describe seeing loved ones who have passed. Describe being welcomed. Describe light and presence. Skeptics call it biology. I understand that. But I have seen it too many times to dismiss."

He folded his hands.

"Here is what forty-six years has taught me. The people who die most peacefully are often the ones who believe they are going somewhere. Not because belief is a drug. Because belief aligns them with something they experience as true. And the ones who die in terror are not always the doubters. Sometimes they are the ones who lived as if death was not real, and now they are confronting it unprepared."

"So you think belief in heaven is functional."

"I think belief in heaven is true," he said. "And because it is true, it functions. Love is stronger than death. Not as poetry. As reality. I have watched it show up over and over. And if you sit with enough dying people, you will see it too."

What I could not dismiss

After three months of reading, I found myself unsettled.

I started this project assuming heaven was primarily a story people tell to soften the terror of death, and among ordinary beliefs, that often seemed true. People reached for heaven the way people reach for a railing when the stairs get steep. Sometimes the railing is solid. Sometimes it is the reach itself that steadies you.

But serious theology was not offering railings. It was offering claims about reality.

Claims that, if true, would mean everything I had documented was incomplete.

I could not prove they were right. I could not prove they were wrong.

Neuroscience does not fully explain consciousness. Even its practitioners admit that the hardest questions remain unresolved. Longing might be explained by evolutionary psychology, or it might be something else. End-of-life experiences might be hallucinations, or they might be glimpses. The resurrection of Jesus might be myth, or it might be history, or it might be something that does not fit cleanly into either category.

I did not know.

What I did know was this.

I had spent eighteen months assuming heaven was a psychological construction. Now I was confronting the possibility that heaven might instead be a structural feature of reality. That death might be an interruption, not a conclusion. That love might be ultimate, and therefore permanent. That longing might point beyond itself.

I could not adopt these beliefs just because they were sophisticated. Sophistication is not truth. But I could no longer reject them simply because I started from disbelief.

I was suspended between materialism I could not fully prove and theology I could not empirically verify. Between those certain heaven does not exist and those certain it does. Between grief I had documented and hope I could not entirely explain away.

And I began to notice something that made me uneasy.

My certainty about uncertainty was its own kind of certainty. My assumption that heaven was constructed might itself be a construction. It might be my version of a life raft, built from skepticism instead of scripture.

If I were going to ask other people to examine their beliefs honestly, then I had to examine mine with the same rigor.

Even if I did not like where that examination might lead.

Chapter 16
What If I'm Wrong

I need to admit something uncomfortable.

I did not begin this project as a neutral observer. I began it convinced that heaven was a story people told themselves to manage their fear of death. I believed I was documenting what others thought, but I was also, quietly, documenting evidence for what I already believed. And without realizing it at first, I selected that evidence carefully.

I interviewed people who doubted. I asked questions designed to surface uncertainty. I paid close attention to the gap between what people said publicly and what they admitted privately.

Unsurprisingly, I found exactly what I was looking for. I found it because I was looking for it.

The priest who admitted he did not know became evidence that religious certainty was performance. The neuroscientist who said "probably" when asked whether consciousness ended became evidence that even science could not be sure. The children who built contradictory versions of heaven became evidence that heaven was a psychological construction rather than a theological truth.

What I did not do was give equal weight to the nun who had experienced God's presence for forty years. I did not spend months reading theologians who had devoted their lives to thinking seriously about resurrection. I did not pause long enough to consider that longing for heaven might point toward something real rather than merely something wished for.

I interviewed more than two hundred people, but I was not collecting data. I was collecting confirmation. Eventually, I had to ask myself why.

I spent eighteen months documenting how religious people perform certainty in order to belong. I wrote about the social pressure to sound faithful, confident, and resolved. What I did not examine was how secular, educated people perform skepticism for the same reason.

My sample was largely urban, educated, and middle-class or above. In those circles, performing doubt about heaven is not brave. It is expected. Saying "I do not know if there is anything after death" functions as a social signal. It communicates intelligence, restraint, and freedom from superstition. It marks you as reasonable.

It serves the same function that "I believe in heaven" serves in evangelical spaces.

Both are performances. Both signal belonging. Both protect identity.

And I documented one while participating fully in the other.

The Gen X participants who said "I do not know" with visible discomfort were performing doubt in much the same way church members expressed certainty. They were saying what their social world allowed them to say. I treated that performance as authenticity while treating religious performance as falsehood.

That distinction was convenient.

It was also dishonest.

Part of what drove this project was my failure with Margaret.

She asked me a question I could not answer honestly, and I felt the weight of that failure long after she died. I told myself this work was about understanding belief, but I began to wonder whether it was also about justification.

What if I needed heaven to be false so my inability to believe in it could feel like wisdom rather than limitation? What if I needed other people's doubt to validate my own? What if this entire project was, at least in part, a defense mechanism disguised as an investigation?

The parents who needed heaven to be real so their children were not truly gone struck me as psychologically motivated.. I documented their need as evidence that the belief was constructed.

But my need for heaven to be false so I did not have to

confront my own disbelief was just as psychological. Just as motivated. Just as protective.

I was doing exactly what I accused believers of doing. I was building a framework to manage fear.

Difference was that my fear was not of death. It was of being wrong.

For years I dismissed C. S. Lewis's argument that longing might be evidence. It sounded circular, almost childish. Wanting something does not make it true. But Lewis was not saying that desire creates reality. He was saying that natural desires correspond to real things.

Hunger points to food. Thirst points to water. Sexual desire points to sex. Curiosity points to truth. And the longing for something beyond this world, for love that does not end, for meaning that survives death, might point toward something real.

Not prove it. Point toward it.

I had spent two years documenting that longing. Children who needed their dead pets to be somewhere. Parents who could not accept that their children no longer existed. Spouses who needed a reunion to remain possible. I treated that longing as pathology, as evidence of humanity's inability to face reality.

But what if longing is not only fear? What if it is perception?

What if they were sensing something I could not sense because I had trained myself not to? What if my inability to long for heaven was not sophistication, but numbness?

I did not know. And I realized I had never truly asked.

Throughout this book, I have written about the performance of certainty. But I need to acknowledge what I performed.

I performed open-minded inquiry while believing the conclusion in advance. I performed neutrality while curating evidence toward a predetermined thesis. I performed intellectual humility while remaining certain that heaven was a psychological construction.

Believers performed faith while doubting. I performed doubt while being certain.

Both avoid the same thing.

Actual uncertainty.

The honest answer to the question "What happens when you die" is not "probably nothing" or "probably something." The honest answer is that I do not know. I cannot know. And neither can anyone else.

Materialists may be right that consciousness ends when the brain stops. Theologians may be right that love is ultimate and death is not final. Both positions have internal logic, and both contain gaps. Neither can be proven from this side of death.

And I had been performing certainty about uncertainty in exactly the same way believers perform certainty about heaven.

So what if I am wrong?

What if N. T. Wright is right, and resurrection is real, and death is interruption rather than conclusion? What if David Bentley Hart is right, and love is fundamental, and therefore continuation is necessary? What if the nun who prayed for forty years was encountering something real? What if the dying patients who described peace were not hallucinating but transitioning? What if the children building heavens were not inventing fantasy but intuiting truth?

I do not know.

That admission, actual admission and not practiced humility, is frightening. Because it means I might have spent two years documenting doubt while missing the possibility of hope. It means the people I assumed were clinging to illusion might have been right in ways they could not articulate. It means my framework, skeptical and grounded in what I could verify, might itself be the construction.

I began this project certain that heaven was a story.

I am ending it uncertain about my certainty.

That uncertainty is not comforting. It does not play well in conversation. It offers no clean conclusions, and it provides no framework for control. It simply sits there, unresolved.

But it is honest.

I do not know what happens when we die. Nobody does.

Believers guess through experience and hope. Skeptics guess through logic and evidence. Both may be right. Both may be wrong. I have no way to determine which.

I cannot undo the bias I brought to this work, and I cannot pretend this was a neutral investigation. But I can name it. I can say clearly that I began believing heaven was false, and that I found evidence that supported that belief because that is what I was searching for.

I can also say that I found things I could not explain. Experiences I could not dismiss. Arguments I could not reduce. Longing I could not fully contain inside psychology.

And I discovered that my certainty about uncertainty was simply another form of certainty. Another performance. Another way of protecting myself from the terror of not knowing.

Now I am left with the same question Margaret asked me.

Do you actually believe that?

The only honest answer I have is this.

I do not know.

I hope there is something. I suspect there is nothing. But I do not know.

And maybe that uncertainty, real uncertainty and not practiced doubt, is the most honest thing I can offer.

PART VI:
HOW TO TALK ABOUT DEATH

Chapter 17

Heaven Is Not A Place

It took me two years and more than two hundred conversations to realize I had been asking the wrong question the entire time.

I had been asking: What is heaven?

As if heaven were a thing that could be described, located, and mapped.

As if the question had an answer that could be uncovered through enough interviews, enough research, enough careful listening.

For many believers, heaven is both a real promise and a source of psychological survival. This book has focused on the second dimension, not to deny the first, but to understand how belief actually functions in people's lives.

Because what I slowly came to see is this.

Heaven is not a thing.

It is not a place.

It is not even, really, a belief.

Heaven is what humans do with the unbearable fact of mortality.

I did not arrive at this insight all at once. There was no revelation, no single conversation that unlocked it. It emerged gradually, through accumulation.

Through watching people construct cosmologies that solved their specific pain rather than described objective reality.

Through noticing that every version of heaven removed what the believer found intolerable and preserved what they could not bear to lose.

Through seeing that belief was rarely about truth in the abstract, and almost always about survival. Psychological survival. Emotional survival. The survival of the ability to keep loving people who die.

Across generations, traditions, and personalities, everyone was doing the same thing.

They were building a response to mortality that made continued life possible. Not afterlife existence, but present life existence.

Because humans cannot truly absorb permanent death. We can say the words. We can understand it intellectually. But we cannot hold it emotionally. We cannot function if we genuinely accept that everyone we love will permanently disappear, and that we will too.

So we create heaven.

Not because we have evidence for it.

But because we have to.

Once I saw this, everything I had collected began to make sense.

Almost no one was primarily concerned with whether their belief was true in some objective, metaphysical sense.

They were concerned with whether it worked.

Whether it helped.

Whether it made life bearable, death less terrifying, and grief survivable.

Heaven was not solving a metaphysical problem.

It was solving a psychological one.

The problem of how to keep living while knowing everyone dies.

The problem of how to love without being destroyed by absence.

The problem of how to face your own mortality without

collapsing into despair.

And heaven, in all its contradictory, evolving, deeply personal forms, was the tool humans had created to solve that problem.

This framework explained everything I had struggled to understand.

Why almost everyone eventually eliminated hell, or at least eternal torment. Because love cannot torture. If heaven is love's construction, it cannot include infinite punishment.

Why reunion mattered so deeply. Because love requires recognition. A heaven where you do not know the people you loved is not heaven at all.

Why have beliefs become customized. Because what I need in order to survive your death is different from what you need to survive mine.

Why did the details keep changing. Because heaven is not a fixed reality we are describing it more accurately over time. It is a tool we keep adapting as our needs evolve.

Why do younger generations seem to need heaven less. Because they had developed other ways to process mortality. Therapy. Community. Meaning-making that did not rely on metaphysics.

Heaven was never primarily about the afterlife.

It was about surviving this life while knowing everyone you love will die.

Eventually, I began asking people a different question.

Not what do you believe about heaven, but what does your belief in heaven allow you to survive?

The answers were remarkably consistent.

It allows me to survive my fear of annihilation. Without heaven, death feels like extinction. With heaven, it feels like a transition.

It allows me to survive injustice. Without heaven, terrible people escape accountability. With heaven, there is reckoning.

It allows me to survive meaninglessness. Without heaven, nothing echoes. With heaven, our choices matter beyond this moment.

It allows me to survive separation. Without heaven, everyone I love eventually disappears. With heaven, we are still moving toward each other.

They were not making claims about geography.

They were describing what they needed in order to keep functioning.

I thought of Rachel, a hospice nurse I interviewed early in the project. She worked with dying patients every day and told me she believed in heaven with complete certainty.

"Not because I can prove it," she said. "But because without it, I could not do this work. I could not watch people die week after week if I thought they were simply ending. I need to believe they are going somewhere. That the love they gave does not vanish. Whether that belief is true or constructed, it allows me to stay present with death without being destroyed by it."

She was not offering theology.

She was describing a survival mechanism that happened to take the shape of heaven.

And maybe that was all heaven had ever been.

That realization forced me to ask the question I had been avoiding.

What do I believe?

Not what I hope.

Not what feels comforting.

Not what sounds intellectually respectable.

What do I actually believe happens when we die?

I tested different answers.

I believe consciousness continues. But did I believe that, or did I just want to?

I believe there is nothing. But did I believe that, or was I trying to be rigorous?

I believe we cannot know. That was true, but it was not a belief. It was an admission of limitation.

None of them felt complete.

So I stopped asking what was correct and asked instead what I needed to be true.

What I need to be true is this.

I need love not to end at death.

Not because it is rational.

Not because I can defend it.

But because I cannot accept that the love I felt for Margaret, the love my daughter feels for me, the love that shapes everything meaningful in human life simply stops when the body stops.

I need Margaret to still exist somehow. Not necessarily as a conscious person in a literal heaven, but as something. A presence. A continuity. A pattern that does not evaporate.

I need consciousness to be more durable than neurons. Not because I have evidence, but because the alternative feels incomplete.

I need death to be a transition rather than erasure. Not only because I am afraid, though I am, but because nothing else in the universe truly ends. Everything transforms. Why would consciousness be the sole exception?

But here is the truth I cannot avoid.

I need these things to be true, but I do not know if they are.

I suspect they are.

I hope they are.

I choose to live as if they are.

But I do not know.

And that uncertainty no longer feels like failure.

After two years of listening, here is what I understand.

Heaven is not where people go when they die.

Heaven is what happens when love refuses to disappear.

That is not a claim about geography or physics or the mechanics of consciousness.

It is a claim about what love does.

Love refuses finality.

Love builds bridges across separation.

Love maintains presence even in absence.

Love creates continuation where none should exist.

Whether that continuation is literal or symbolic, metaphysical or emotional, I do not know.

But I know this.

Love does not accept death as the final word.

And that refusal is heaven.

The Christian names it with resurrection and reunion.

The Hindu names it with reincarnation and karma.

The Buddhist names it with dissolution into consciousness.

The Muslim names it with gardens and peace.

The secular person names it with legacy and memory.

The child names it with creative mode where nobody can hurt you.

Different language.

Different certainty.

Same insistence.

Love does not end.

This understanding did not give me answers.

It did not tell me what actually happens after death.

It did not resolve the question of consciousness.

It did not prove or disprove religion.

But it gave me something better.

Understanding.

I understood why people needed heaven even when they doubted it.

I understood why honesty about belief was so difficult.

I understood what heaven was actually doing.

And I understood what I believed, not as knowledge, but as necessity.

I needed love to persist.

I needed Margaret to still matter, still exist in some way I could not explain.

I needed death not to erase meaning.

Whether reality will meet those needs, I do not know.

But I know I am not alone in having them.

Every person I spoke with, regardless of belief, was wrestling with the same thing.

We all need death not to be final.

We all need love to continue.

And heaven, in all its imperfect and contradictory forms, is how humans respond to that need.

Heaven is not something you know.

It is something you need.

And maybe needing it is enough.

Maybe longing itself is the answer.

Not proof of an afterlife, but proof that love refuses endings.

That refusal, that insistence, that ache for continuation, whether it creates reality or simply responds to it, is what makes us human.

And it is what keeps us alive while everyone we love is dying.

Chapter 18

The Map Is Not The Territory

Three weeks after finishing the manuscript, I received an email from Patricia, the woman from the Gen X chapter who had told me she no longer believed in heaven but could not tell anyone.

"My mother died yesterday," she wrote. "And I need to tell you what happened."

We met at the same coffee shop where we had spoken months earlier. She looked exhausted in the particular way people do after a loved one dies, that mix of grief and relief and emotional whiplash that arrives when waiting finally ends.

"Tell me," I said.

"Two days before she died, she was lucid. More lucid than she had been in weeks. She looked at me and said, Patricia, I need to ask you something, and I need you to be honest."

Patricia paused, stirring coffee she was not drinking.

She asked, "Do you believe I am going to heaven?"

"What did you say?"

"I panicked. Because this was the moment I had been afraid of my whole life. The moment where I would have to choose between lying to comfort her or telling the truth and risking her peace. I opened my mouth to lie, to give her the answer she needed to hear."

"But you didn't."

"I started to. Then I stopped. Because I realized she did not ask if I believe in heaven. She asked if I believe she is going to heaven. And those are not the same question."

"So what did you say?"

"I told her this: Mom, I do not know what happens after we die. I wish I did. But I know this. If there is any justice in the universe, if there is any mercy, if love means anything at all, then yes, you are going to a place where you are whole and at peace and free from pain. And whether that place is called heaven or something else, whether it is literal or something we cannot even imagine, I believe you are going to be okay."

Patricia was crying now, quietly.

"She smiled. Not a polite smile. A real one. And she said, that is all I needed to know. Not what is true. Just that you believe I will be okay. Then she closed her eyes. Two days later, she died."

She looked at me directly.

"You were right about the silence. About what it costs us. I spent my life performing certainty I did not feel, afraid to speak honestly. And when it finally mattered most, when my mother was dying and needed to know I cared, I told her the truth. And it was enough."

I thought about her words for weeks.

She had not lied.

She had not claimed certainty.

She had found something better.

Honest hope.

Not "heaven is definitely real and you are definitely going there."

Not "there is probably nothing but I will pretend otherwise."

Just this: I do not know, but I believe you will be okay.

And somehow, that had been enough.

Three months later, the website I had created had grown to more than five thousand submissions.

Five thousand people sharing what they believed, what they doubted, what they feared, what they hoped.

Five thousand different maps of heaven.

Reading them, I saw the same truth everywhere.

We are all doing our best with an impossible question.

We are all building meaning in the face of mortality.

We are all constructing hope where despair would be easier.

We are all refusing to accept that death is final, even when we cannot prove that it is not.

I kept thinking about Margaret.

About how she had asked me what I believed and I had given her the script instead of the truth.

About how I had failed her by performing certainty when what she needed was honesty.

About how we had decades of friendship, yet never once talked openly about what we thought happened after death until she had three weeks left to live.

So I wrote her a letter.

Not because I thought she would read it.

But because there were things I still needed to say.

Margaret,

I am sorry I gave you the script instead of the truth when you asked what I believed. I am sorry I wasted our last real conversation on words that sounded comforting but were empty.

I spent two years asking more than two hundred people what they believe about heaven, and I am more uncertain now than when

I started.

Some days I think consciousness continues. Some days I think death is final. Most days I just miss you and wish I could ask what you think now that you know.

I tell people that heaven is what happens when love refuses to disappear. That it is not a place, but a persistence. That your influence continues in everyone you touched.

When I say it, it sounds true. It sounds like I have learned something.

But I do not know if believing your love persists in me is the same thing as believing you still exist.

If you are somewhere, if consciousness continues, if you can somehow know what I have done with the question you asked me, I hope you are not disappointed that I still do not have an answer.

And if you are nowhere, if death was final, then I am writing this to myself, to the memory of you that still lives in me.

I do not know if that is enough to call heaven.

But it is what I have.

Thank you for asking.

I posted the letter on the website anonymously.

Within an hour, fifty people responded with letters of their own. Within a week, five hundred.

People writing to parents.

To children.

To spouses.

To friends.

People speaking into silence and trusting that speaking still mattered, even if no one could answer back.

And I realized something.

This was what heaven had always been about.

Not the afterlife itself.

But the belief that speaking to the dead matters. That love continues even when the other person cannot respond. That connection does not vanish just because breath stops.

Near the end of this project, a hospice chaplain in Oregon emailed me. She told me she had begun reading submissions from the website to her patients.

"Not the ones who want certainty," she wrote. "They already have that. But the ones who do not know and are terrified to admit it. I read them words from people who also do not know. And it helps. Not because it gives answers. Because it gives permission."

Permission to die uncertain.

That phrase stayed with me.

Because I had spent this entire project believing I was mapping belief systems, cataloging what people think about heaven.

But maybe what I was actually doing was offering permission.

Permission to not know.

Permission to doubt.

Permission to hope without pretending certainty.

Permission to die the way Margaret died. Honestly.

Three years after she asked me what I believed, I still do not have certainty.

But I have understanding.

Heaven is not a place we go when we die.

Heaven is what love builds to survive death.

Some people build it from scripture.

Some from tradition.

Some from memory.

Some from philosophy.

But everyone builds it.

Because humans cannot live if we truly accept that everyone

we love will permanently disappear.

Belief does not need to be true to be meaningful.

But it does need to be humane.

A belief in heaven that comforts a grieving parent helps.

A belief in heaven that allows the dying to face death with less terror helps.

A belief in heaven that shames, excludes, or condemns harms.

The question is not "Is it true?"

The question is "Does it help us love better and die easier?"

Faith is not the absence of doubt.

Faith is choosing meaning despite doubt.

I choose to believe love continues.

I choose to believe death is a transition, not erasure.

I choose to believe the people I have lost are not entirely gone.

Not because I know these things are true.

But choosing them makes me more capable of love, more present in grief, and more willing to live fully in a world that offers no guarantees.

Three years later, standing at Margaret's grave, I do not need to feel her presence to know she remains.

She is in how I speak honestly now.

She is in how I approach uncertainty.

She is in this book, in every conversation that exists because she asked one question I could not answer.

That is heaven.

Not a place.

Not a reward.

Not even necessarily a belief.

Just what love does when it refuses to disappear.

And it is real.

And it is enough.

Chapter 19

How We Talk Now

At the first funeral I attended after starting this project, I found myself counting the phrases.

“She is in a better place now.” Seven times.

“God needed another angel.” Four times.

“She is not suffering anymore.” Eleven times.

“You will see her again someday.” Six times.

“Everything happens for a reason.” Three times.

No one said, this is terrible and unfair and I have no idea what to say to make it better.

No one said, I am so sorry.

No one acknowledged the actual reality of the moment, which was that a fifty-three-year-old woman had died of cancer and her husband and children were shattered.

Instead, everyone performed comfort.

They followed the script.

And the script required pretending death was not as devastating as it felt, because the person was supposedly somewhere better now.

I watched the husband nod mechanically as person after person told him his wife was in heaven. I watched him say thank you again and again. And I wondered whether anyone had given him permission to be angry. To say this was unbearable. To admit that no place without her could possibly be better.

The script does not allow for that kind of honesty.

The script demands acceptance. Hope. Faith that everything will be okay, even when everything is not okay.

Why We Use the Script

I interviewed a woman named Jennifer whose mother had died six months earlier. When I asked what people said at the funeral, she sighed.

"All the usual things. She is at peace. She is with God. She is watching over you. You will see her again."

"Did any of it help?"

"No," she said. "It made me feel more alone."

When I asked why, she thought for a moment.

"Because they were not talking about my mother. They were talking about some version of her that existed inside their beliefs. They were managing their own discomfort. And I had to pretend it helped."

What would have helped, she said, was simple.

"Someone saying, this is awful. I am so sorry. Tell me about her. That is it. Just acknowledgment that the loss was real and I was allowed to feel it."

The script exists because death makes us uncomfortable. We do not know how to sit with someone else's pain without trying to fix it. So we reach for familiar phrases, things we have heard before, things that sound kind even when they are hollow.

We hope the words will fill the silence.

But they do not fill it. They cover it.

They allow us to avoid the real conversation, which is this: this is terrible. I cannot fix it. I am here anyway.

The Man Who Stopped Performing

I met Peter at a coffee shop in Oak Park. He was sixty-two. His wife had died of ALS eight months earlier.

"Did people tell you she was in a better place?"

"Constantly."

"Did it help?"

"It made me want to scream," he said. "She was not in a better place. She was dead. And I was alone. And everyone kept pretending that was somehow good news."

For the first six months, he played along. He said thank you. He nodded. He let people believe their words were helping.

"It was easier than telling the truth."

Eventually, he stopped.

Someone told him his wife was in heaven watching over him, and he replied, "I do not believe that. I think she is gone. And pretending she is somewhere else does not help me."

The reaction was immediate.

"They looked horrified," he said. "Like I had broken some sacred rule. They rushed to reassure me that she was definitely in heaven. And I just said, maybe. But I do not know that. And I am not going to pretend I do."

After that, something changed.

"Once I stopped performing, other people got honest too. People admitted they did not know what to say. People admitted they had doubts. The conversations became real."

When I asked what he wished people had said, he did not hesitate.

"I wish they had said, this is unfair and terrible and I do not have words. I wish they had asked about her. Who she was. What I missed. I wish they had acknowledged how bad this was instead of trying to make it smaller."

His advice was simple.

"Do not use the script. Do not offer theology to make yourself feel better. Just say I am sorry and listen."

What My Daughter Asked

My daughter was seventeen when I began this project. One evening she overheard me talking about it and asked what I was doing.

I told her I was asking people what they believed about heaven.

She thought for a moment, then said, "What if you do not believe in heaven? Is it lying if you say someone is in heaven at a funeral?"

"Yes," I said. "If you do not believe it and you say it anyway, that is lying."

"So what are you supposed to say?"

I told her you could say you were sorry. You could say you missed the person. You could ask about them. You could sit quietly with someone who was hurting.

"But what if someone asks you directly?" she said. "What if

they ask if you think their person is in heaven?"

I thought about Margaret. About that moment she asked me if I actually believed. About how I had lied.

"You can say you do not know," I said. "You can say different people believe different things. And you can say what you do know, which is that the person was loved and that love is real."

She frowned. "That is not the script."

"No," I said. "It is better than the script. It is honest."

Breaking the Script

After talking to Peter, I began experimenting at funerals.

Instead of saying they were in a better place, I said, "This is a profound loss."

Instead of offering beliefs, I asked, "Tell me about them."

Instead of promising reunion, I said, "I am so sorry."

The reactions varied.

Some people looked relieved, as if they had been waiting for permission to grieve without pretending everything was okay.

Some looked confused, as if I had violated an unspoken contract.

Others filled the space with honesty they had been holding

back.

At one funeral, a woman responded to "This is a profound loss" with fifteen minutes of truth. About how complicated her relationship with her father had been. How angry she still was. How exhausting it was to hear people praise him when she was still hurting.

Afterward, she thanked me.

"Everyone else kept saying he is in heaven like that fixes everything," she said. "You were the only one who acknowledged that this is hard."

At another funeral, an elderly man named Thomas approached me after I had said simply, "I am so sorry for your loss."

"I believe my wife is with God," he said. "I believe that with my whole heart. But what helps me is not when people tell me that as if it fixes my grief. What helps is when someone acknowledges that even with that belief, I am devastated. That even if she is in heaven, I am still here without her. And that is unbearable."

He paused.

"Belief does not erase grief. It just gives it a different shape. I wish more people understood that."

What Honest Language Looks Like

After two years of funerals and grief conversations, I learned what actually helps.

Not theology.

Not certainty.

Not the script.

What helps is honesty.

Honest language requires abandoning performance. It requires admitting what you do not know. It requires allowing uncertainty without shame. It requires witnessing pain without trying to solve it. It requires offering presence instead of explanation.

It also requires clearer language, especially with children. Saying "died" instead of "passed away." Saying "dead" instead of "gone somewhere better."

And when you share a belief, share it as a belief.

I believe.

I hope.

Not: I know.

This is harder than using the script. The script is easy. It is socially approved. It protects us from vulnerability.

But it does not help the grieving. It protects the living.

Talking to Children

A grief counselor named Maria told me that one of the worst things adults do is lie to children about death.

"They say, Mommy went to sleep," she told me, "and then the child is afraid to go to sleep. Or they say, Daddy went on a trip, and the child waits for him to come home. Or they say, God needed another angel, and the child becomes angry at God for taking their parent."

Children take language literally.

When you say someone is watching over them, they imagine surveillance. When you say heaven is better, they wonder why their parent chose it over staying with them.

"The truth is kinder," Maria said. "Your parent died. Their body stopped working. They are not coming back. And that is very sad."

Children can handle honesty. What they cannot handle is deception.

The Silence Around Death

Over two years, I learned that the silence around death causes more harm than any belief or disbelief about heaven.

People need permission to speak honestly. Permission to doubt. Permission to grieve without platitudes. Permission to say "I do not know" without being corrected.

Breaking that silence is not about replacing one script with another.

It is about making space.

A space where grief can be witnessed instead of managed.

A space where uncertainty can be admitted instead of hidden.

A space where love can be expressed without requiring metaphysical certainty.

That space is what people need most.

Not answers.

Not fixes.

Not comfort phrases that make death smaller.

Just an honest company while facing what cannot be fixed.

Chapter 20

What Actually Helps

After two hundred conversations about death, and two years of attending funerals with a new kind of attention, I started keeping notes on a different question. Not what people said they believed about heaven, but what actually helped them survive the days and months after someone died.

Not what we assume helps. Not what we repeat because it sounds comforting. What grieving people told me helped.

This chapter is practical. It is meant to be used. Because the next time someone you know loses someone, you will feel the familiar panic of not knowing what to say. The script will be right there, ready to rescue you from awkward silence. This chapter is an alternative to the script.

At funerals: what to say

At funerals, most people reach for phrases that attempt to make death less sharp. The problem is that grieving people do not need the moment softened. They need it acknowledged.

Avoid the standard lines. Do not say they are in a better place. Do not say God needed another angel. Do not say everything happens for a reason. Do not say they are not suffering anymore, or you will see them again, or at least they lived a long life, or at least you had time to say goodbye, or time heals all wounds. Even when those lines are well meant, they often land as minimization. They also tend to be about the speaker's discomfort more than the mourner's pain.

Say simpler things. Say, I am so sorry. Say, this is a terrible loss. Say, I do not have the right words, but I am here. Ask, tell me about them. Ask, what do you miss most? Offer something specific: I loved how they did that thing where… If you are close enough to do more than speak, ask, what do you need right now? and be prepared to follow through.

The difference is not eloquence. It is honesty. You are acknowledging that the loss is real and that it hurts.

If you feel compelled to reference belief, make it personal instead of declarative. Do not state what you cannot know. Instead of "They are in heaven now," say something like: I believe we will see each other again, and that belief helps me. But right now, I am just so sorry you are going through this. Or, I do not know what happens after death, but I know they mattered, and I know you are hurting. The point is not to smuggle theology into the moment. The point is to stay with the grief.

What grieving people need, according to grieving people

I asked fifty people who had lost someone in the past year what actually helped. Their answers were remarkably consistent.

What helped most was not clever language. It was action. People who showed up without needing instruction. People who brought food. People who did specific tasks without asking for permission first: mowing the lawn, walking the dog, picking up children from school, handling errands, and sitting in the house so the grieving person was not alone. Listening without advice. Letting them cry without trying to stop it. Saying the person's name. Sharing specific memories. Remembering them weeks and months later, when everyone else had moved on. Sitting in silence when there was nothing to say.

What did not help was also consistent. Let me know if you need anything, which sounds generous and often becomes an excuse to do nothing. Unrequested theology. Instructions about how they should feel. Comparisons that shrink their loss. Disappearing because you do not know what to say. Avoiding the dead person's name out of fear that it will remind them, as if they could forget. Expecting them to be over it in a few months.

The pattern was clear. Presence is better than advice. Action is better than words. Honesty is better than platitudes. And most grieving people need permission to grieve for as long as they grieve.

Talking to children about death

Every grief counselor I spoke with said some version of the same thing. Children do not need euphemisms. They need truth, delivered in language that matches their age.

Use clear, direct words. Grandma died. Not passed away, not lost, not gone to sleep, not gone on a journey. Explain in concrete terms: Her body stopped working. And when necessary, say the hardest line plainly: She is not coming back.

Answer questions honestly, which often means admitting what you do not know. If a child asks, where is she now? You can say, I do not know. Some people believe in heaven. Some people believe other things. What I know is her body stopped working and she died, and we miss her. If they ask, can she see me? You can say, I do not know. Some people believe that. Some people do not. What I do know is that she loved you very much when she was alive. If they ask, will I die? tell the truth without terrifying them: Someday, yes. Everyone dies eventually. But most people live a very long time. You are safe right now, and I am here to take care of you.

Let children grieve the way children grieve. They often do it in bursts. They might cry and then go play five minutes later. They might ask the same question repeatedly. They might blame themselves. They might become angry. Do not rush them out of it. Answer honestly each time. Do not tell them how they should feel.

Avoid the common lies that create unintended harm. Saying

someone is sleeping can create fear of sleep. Saying God needed another angel can create anger at God. Saying someone went on a trip creates false hope. Hiding your own grief teaches them grief is shameful. Refusing to talk about the person teaches them that the person is now a forbidden topic.

Do the opposite. Use the person's name. Share memories. Look at the photos. Let children ask questions. Cry with them when you need to. Create small rituals: lighting a candle, visiting a grave, cooking a favorite meal, celebrating a birthday. Tell them it is okay to be sad and it is also okay to laugh.

Talking to dying parents

This is one of the hardest conversations we avoid, often until it is too late. I interviewed thirty people who had dying parents. Most admitted they tried to keep everything positive until there was no time left. The ones who spoke honestly, even imperfectly, said the conversation was painful but essential.

Start plainly. You do not need a perfect opening, only courage. You can say, I need to talk to you about something difficult. I know you are dying, and I do not want us to spend our remaining time pretending you are not. Can we talk about it?

Then ask the questions people tend to avoid. What are you most afraid of? What do you need from me right now? Is there anything unfinished between us that we should address? What do you want me to remember? What do you believe happens after you die? How can I help you die the way you want to die?

And say what matters. I love you. Thank you for… with specifics. I am going to miss you. I am scared too. It is okay to let go when you are ready.

Avoid the lines that deny reality or pressure them into performing strength. Do not say you are going to be fine. They are dying. Do not say do not talk like that. Do not say you have to fight, as if death is a moral failure. Do not reach for everything happens for a reason, which is philosophy at the worst possible moment.

If they ask what you believe about the afterlife, be honest, and frame it as a belief rather than certainty. I believe we will see each other again. I hope that is true. But I do not know. What I know is I love you and I am here with you now. Or, I do not know what happens after death, but I know you mattered to me. And that will not end when you die.

The key is realness. Do not perform certainty you do not have. They are dying. They already know what is real. They need you to be real too.

When someone says something harmful

Sometimes people say things that are not only unhelpful but actively painful. God never gives you more than you can handle. At least you can have more children. They lived a full life.

You are allowed to correct people. You can do it gently and clearly. I know you are trying to help, but that does not help me right now. What helps is just knowing you care. Or, I appreciate you being here, but I would rather just talk about them. Can you tell me a memory you have? Or, that phrase is painful for me. Can we just sit together instead?

You do not owe anyone gratitude for platitudes that hurt. You are allowed to ask for what you need.

Long-term support

Grief does not end after the funeral. It changes shape, but it persists for months and years. Many people told me the worst part of grief was not the first week, when everyone showed up. It was the third month, the sixth month, the first year, when the world had moved on and they were still carrying the loss.

What helps long-term is simple, and rare. People who check in later. People who remember the birthday, the anniversary, and the date of death. People who still say the person's name. People who do not treat grief as a problem that should have been solved by now. People who understand that grief comes in waves.

Specific actions matter. Text on hard days: Thinking of you today. I know this is the anniversary. I am here. Share a memory without being asked: I was thinking about them today. I remembered when they… It made me smile. Invite them to things even if they say no. Do not avoid them because you do not know what to say. Ask about the person in ordinary conversation: What would they think about this? Or what do you think they would say right now?

What does not help is also predictable. Disappearing after the funeral. Avoiding the topic entirely. Saying you must be over it by now. Telling them to move on. Offering unsolicited grief advice. Comparing their loss to yours. Making their grief about you.

The most important thing

After two years of research, the most important thing I learned was simple.

Grieving people do not need you to fix their grief. They need you to witness it.

A woman named Linda told me about the friend who helped her most after her son died. "She didn't say anything about heaven. She didn't tell me he was in a better place. She didn't offer me any comforting beliefs. She just showed up every Tuesday for six months. She sat with me. She let me cry. She listened to me tell the same stories about him over and over. And when I couldn't talk, she just sat there with me in the silence. That saved my life."

That is what helps.

Not theology. Not the script. Not clever words.

Just showing up. Just staying. Just witnessing what cannot be fixed.

They do not need answers about heaven. They need permission to not have answers.

They do not need theology. They need presence.

They do not need the script. They need honesty.

Show up. Say you are sorry. Listen. Do practical things. Remember the person. Let them grieve for as long as they grieve.

That is what helps.

Everything else is performance.

Chapter 21
What I Would Tell Margaret Now

Margaret,

It has been two and a half years since you asked me that question. Two and a half years since you looked at me in the hospice room and said, "Do you actually believe that?"

I gave you the script. I told you I believed you were going to heaven. I said you would see your husband again. I said all the things I thought I was supposed to say.

You looked at me like you knew I was lying.

Because I was.

I did not believe it. Not really. I wanted to believe it. I hoped it might be true. But when you asked me directly, in that moment, I could not give you the truth. I gave you what I thought would comfort you instead.

And then you died.

I could not stop thinking about that moment. About how I had failed you by not being honest. About how the script had gotten in the way of a real connection. About how I did not actually know what I believed about heaven because I had never forced myself to examine it.

So I spent the next two years asking people what they really believed. Not what they were supposed to believe. Not what their religion taught. What they actually thought happened when someone died.

I spoke with priests and nurses, atheists and theologians, children and the elderly, people who were grieving and people who were dying. I asked the same question again and again, trying to understand what people reached for when certainty fell away.

And now I have an answer for you.

Not an answer about heaven. I still do not know anything definitive about heaven. But I do have an answer to the question you asked me.

Do I actually believe that?

Here is what I believe now, Margaret.

I believe consciousness is stranger than we understand. I believe the materialists might be right that it ends when the brain stops. But I also believe they might be wrong. We do not actually know what consciousness is or where it comes from, and that not knowing leaves room for possibility.

I believe love is real in a way that goes beyond chemistry and survival. I believe the connection between people is more than memory or biology alone. I believe what we build together matters in ways that do not simply vanish when a body stops breathing.

I believe that if there is any justice in the universe, any mercy, any meaning beyond randomness, then yes, you are somewhere. Not necessarily a heaven of clouds and harps, but somewhere. Some continuation of what made you yourself. Some persistence of the love you gave and received.

But I cannot prove any of this.

And I am not certain.

I have learned that certainty is not what matters.

What matters is how I live with the uncertainty.

Do I live as if nothing matters because everything ends, or do I live as if love has weight, connection carries responsibility, and what we do here leaves a mark that does not disappear simply because our bodies do?

I chose the second.

Not because I can prove it, but because that choice makes me more capable of love. More present with people. More willing to invest in relationships that may someday end but matter anyway.

If I am wrong, I will never know.

If I am right, I will have lived aligned with something true.

So when you asked me, "Do you actually believe that?" the honest answer should have been this.

I believe you mattered.

I believe what you built in this life continues in everyone you touched.

I believe the love between you and your husband is real in a way that may transcend death.

I do not know if you will see him again.

I hope you will.

I choose to live as if that hope has meaning.

But I do not know.

And then I should have asked you what you believed.

Because your belief mattered more than mine. Your way of facing your own death mattered more than my theology or my attempt to offer comfort I did not actually possess.

I should have given you space to speak honestly about your fear, your hope, your doubt. I should have sat with you inside the uncertainty instead of covering it with rehearsed certainty.

I failed you in that moment, Margaret. Not because I did not believe in heaven strongly enough, but because I was not honest with you.

And I am sorry.

If I could do it again, I would sit beside you and say, “I do not know what happens. I have things I hope are true, but I do not know. Tell me what you are afraid of. Tell me what you hope for. Let us be honest with each other about this impossible thing we are facing.”

And then I would listen.

I would not try to fix your uncertainty with my certainty. I would stay with you inside it.

That is what I learned from two hundred conversations. Not what happens when we die, but how to be with people who are dying without letting the script get in the way.

I learned that presence matters more than theology. That witnessing pain helps more than minimizing it. That saying “I do not know” can be more comforting than offering certainty you do not actually have.

I learned that people do not need answers. They need company while they face what cannot be answered.

I learned this too late to help you.

But maybe telling your story hclpcd somconc clsc. Maybe people who read this will do better than I did when someone they love is dying. Maybe they will be honest instead of performing.

Maybe they will witness instead of fixing. Maybe they will stay instead of reaching for platitudes.

If they do, then maybe something good came from my failure with you.

I think about you often. I wonder if you are somewhere. I wonder if you found out the answer to the question none of us can answer while living. I wonder if there was something after that last breath, or if it simply ended, or if the question itself was framed wrong.

I will not know until I die. If then.

But I do know this.

You shaped me. The question you asked started something that changed how I think about death, honesty, and connection. The love you gave your husband, your children, your friends lives on in how they live and what they choose and the shape they leave on the world.

That is real, whether or not there is a heaven.

And if there is a heaven, if there is any continuation at all, then I believe you are there. Not because I can prove it, but because I choose to live as if the universe has that kind of grace in it.

You asked me what I believed.

I believe you mattered.

I believe love is real.

I believe consciousness may continue in ways we do not understand.

I believe the question you asked was more important than any answer I could have given.

And I believe that two and a half years later, I have finally told you the truth.

I miss you, Margaret.

Thank you for asking the question I could not answer.

It changed everything.

And maybe that is all any of us can do.

Ask the questions that have no answers.

Love the people who will die.

Stay present in the uncertainty.

And refuse to let death have the final word.

Even when we do not know what comes next.

About The Author

Shehzad Amlani is a writer and entrepreneur trained to look for patterns, data, and answers that hold up under scrutiny. But no framework prepared him for the question his friend Margaret asked on her deathbed: "Do you actually believe I'm going to heaven?"

In that moment, he realized he had been offering comfort without knowing whether he truly believed it himself.

Over the next two years, he spoke with more than 200 people across different faiths, generations, and belief systems, including Christians, Muslims, Jews, Buddhists, atheists, hospice workers, dying patients, grieving parents, and children. He asked a simple question that rarely has a simple answer: What do you actually believe happens after we die?

What he found wasn't certainty or consensus. It was something more complex and more human. People who believed deeply but questioned privately. People who doubted openly but still hoped. People who carried both faith and uncertainty at the same time.

His work explores that space between belief and doubt, where honest questions matter more than easy answers, and where love sometimes means admitting you don't know.

The Heaven Question is his first book.

www.ingramcontent.com/pod-product-compliance
Lightning Source LLC
LaVergne TN
LVHW010608100826
845148LV00014B/2890